Chuck Gallagher's book, *Second Chances*, offers every reader hard-hitting, no-nonsense life tools that each of us can manifest into the power of choice intelligence and its many benefits. This is not another, "Here's my story and what I've learned" book. It's much more. It's a book that says "Take what I've learned and apply it in your life. You will transform your destiny to a higher level of consciousness through better choices and higher purpose!" It's a call to action that doesn't mince words.

Chuck brilliantly demonstrates in this book that life is full of grit that can become imbedded in our soul—just like the grain of sand that embeds itself within the oyster's shell—the grit of life, its challenges, heartbreak, and pain, also can be transformed into a beautiful pearl within us all. *Second Chances* guides the reader through Chuck's personal story of triumph to finding his or her own rare, one-of-a-kind pearl within. Chuck's story illustrates how imprisonment of the soul can take place behind bars or outside of them. It's a choice we can make and then change the trajectory of life when we make it.

As Chuck says so eloquently in this book, "You may make a mistake, but you are not a mistake." Not to read *Second Chances*, in my opinion, would be a mistake I strongly recommend avoiding.

—Anne Bruce
International speaker and bestselling author of *Discover True North: A 4-Week Approach to Ignite Your Passion and Activate Your Potential; Be Your Own Mentor; How to Motivate Every Employee; Speak for A Living; and more.*

Chuck Gallagher's *Second Chances* is a life progressing book with an important message about making the right choices. Make the right choice and read it.

—Dean Lindsay
Author of *The Progress Challenge and Cracking the Networking CODE*

Chuck Gallagher is one of those people who, when you meet them in person, you instantly like. So it comes as a big surprise when you hear his story. He's not the stereotype of an ex-con, and perhaps that's one reason why it's hard to put this book down. Chuck has told the ugly part of his poor choices and how he learned his lessons the hard way, so that all of the rest of us can consider each choice we make and avoid life-changing mistakes. The good news is Chuck learned to make great choices—like sharing his story to inspire others. This book will make you think, and it could save lives.

—Lorri Allen

Talk Show Host, *Mornings* with Lorri and Larry

Second Chances shows you how to make better first choices. It is one of those rare books that effectively bridges the gap between personal accountability and business success. Read it. Heed it. Apply its lessons.

—Randy G. Pennington

Author of *Results Rule! Build a Culture that Blows the Competition Away*

This touching story of real-life circumstances blends the wisdom of experience with a powerful insight for successful living.

—Dr. NidoQubein

President, High Point University
Chairman, Great Harvest Bread Co.

Chuck Gallagher offers his readers a short cut past the frailties of the human condition. His narrative comes to life in a substantive and fascinating manner. Why learn the hard way when Chuck has done it for you? The first chance you get, read this book and live life to the fullest.

—Vince Poscente

New York Times bestselling author of *The Age of Speed*

SECOND CHANCES

SECOND CHANCES

TRANSFORMING ADVERSITY INTO OPPORTUNITY

Chuck Gallagher

BROWN BOOKS
PUBLISHING GROUP

SECOND CHANCES
TRANSFORMING ADVERSITY INTO OPPORTUNITY

© 2010 Chuck Gallagher

"Trust His Heart." Written by Eddie Carswell & Babbie Mason copyright ©1989 by Word Music, Inc. (ASCAP)/May Sun Music (Admin, by Word Music, Inc.) (ASCAP)/ Dayspring Music, Inc. (BMI)/ Causing Clance Music (Admin. by Dayspring, Music) (BMI) All rights reserved. Used with permission.

Scripture quotations are taken from the Holy Bible, English Standard Version, copyright © 2001 by Crossway Bibles, a division of Good News Publishers.

Manufactured in the United States of America.

For information, please contact:

Brown Books Publishing Group
16200 North Dallas Parkway, Suite 170
Dallas, Texas 75248
www.brownbooks.com
972-381-0009

A New Era in Publishing™

ISBN-13: 978-1-934812-43-3
ISBN-10: 1-934812-43-9

LCCN: 2010934695

www.chuckgallagher.com

This book is dedicated to my two sons, Rob and Alex, whose love glows in my life and to those who saw value in me when I didn't see value in myself.

Table of Contents

Foreword

The quote, "Prosperity is a great teacher, adversity is a greater..." is a powerful lesson that at first glance also sums up Chuck Gallagher's soulful expression of life before, during and after his incarceration and is poignantly spoken from the heart in his new book, *Second Chances: Transforming Adversity Into Opportunity.* Just like the English writer, William Hazlitt, who penned the powerful quote on adversity and it's flip side, Gallagher takes an equally humanistic and real-world approach to this message with his easy and relatable writing style.

Gallagher's *Second Chances,* begs of the reader to examine and question some of the following ideas: "Are you making the most of yourself now that you've been given that second or third, or even fourth chance in life?" "What are you doing with the good fortune and prosperity bestowed upon you in this lifetime?" "Are you repeating old habits and then wondering why you are where you are?" Or, "Do you truly realize that you are where you are because of the choices that you've made in this lifetime and that when you alter your choices, you can alter the trajectory of your life, forever?"

This book drives home the critical importance of using our intellect as well as our inner wisdom, or as I call it, true north, to make better choices along the way. It's important to note that Gallagher's book is not just another story of hard lessons learned and redemption realized.

It's much more, because it brings decision-making and choice-making to the forefront of our conscious behavior and points us in the direction, via our inner compass, to a better, more fulfilling and worthwhile life. Gallagher then takes this concept a step further by underscoring the importance of individual accountability and suggests to the reader that choice isn't just a decision, right or wrong, good or bad, instead it's way beyond that. It's an emotional intelligence, an inner compass of strength and a navigational tool to help us find our way out of hard times and dark places.

Gallagher makes it clear through his own shortcomings and personal endurance that what happened to him and the position he found himself in—convicted of a felony—was no accident, or even something out of his control. He later comes to realize, through the most difficult of circumstances, that each of us is in control of our own destiny and that we design our lives based on the choices we make. Winston Churchill said, "We create our own universe as we go along." In many ways, Chuck sends a similar and striking message in this book, pointing to foibles and mistakes we all make but distinguishing clearly between being human and making mistakes, to not thinking of ourselves as mistakes. This is an *aha* moment for the reader near the conclusion of the book.

This book is a call to action and that's why I read it in its entirety. Gallagher shows us the way and warns the reader of creating a prison of his or her own choosing. He states that, yes, he experienced physical prison, but how many of us live in prisons we create because of how we think, choose, love, hate, or experience life? This book brilliantly illustrates how imprisonment of the soul can take place behind bars or outside of them. *Second Chances* offers nuts and bolts, hard-hitting, no-nonsense tools that you as the reader can actually manifest into the power of choice intelligence. This book says loudly, take what I've learned and apply it in your life and you will transform your destiny, every God-given opportunity and, in the process, you'll develop a higher level of consciousness through better choices and a higher purpose.

Gallagher conveys the feeling that perhaps life is full of grit that can easily become imbedded in the soul—just like the grain of sand that embeds itself within the oyster's shell—the grit of life, it's challenges, heartbreak, and pain, also can be transformed into a beautiful pearl within us all. Second Chances guides the reader through Chuck's personal story of triumph to finding his or her own rare, one-of-a-kind pearl within.

Shortly before his sixth month in prison, Gallagher says to himself, "Where from here?" This ultimately becomes the call to action upon which this book is premised. As the author says, "You may make a mistake, but you are not a mistake." So what's next? What do you do next? How will you put one foot in front of the other to manifest the power of the choices you make now and in the future?

When you've finished reading Second Chances, my feeling is, you'll have a good idea about where from here is and how to get there.

—Anne Bruce

International Speaker and Bestselling Author of
Discover True North: A 4-Week Approach to Ignite Your Passion and Activate Your Potential; Be Your Own Mentor; How to Motivate Every Employee; Speak for A Living; and more.

Preface

✦

As human beings born into this spiritual and physical life on earth, we have been given the greatest gift in existence—the gift is "FREE WILL." We may not know from day to day what the outcome our choices might yield, but I have come to know that there are no mistakes. It was no mistake that my path crossed that of Chuck Gallagher, author of this book.

No individual has ever been created as a puppet! Once we reach the age of reason and are fully mature, we form our own nature, our own attitude, and all of our own physical and spiritual abilities to become an independent individual. Although, all those around us as well as the environment in which we are born influence us, we are free to maximize the gifts of life we have been given. The freedom of choice is powerful and the decisions we make daily shape our destiny.

The key ingredient is "FREE WILL." We are creatures with intelligence that can differentiate between right and wrong. We're not controlled strictly by instinct; rather we can understand the difference between good and evil, between right and wrong. We do enjoy a conscience that motivates us by the realization of the natural law of "CONSEQUENCES." It is true, "every choice has a consequence" as Chuck outlines so well in this book.

Once the natural law of "CONSEQUENCES" is removed, there is no incentive to control and discipline our use of the other great gifts we have been given. Those gifts are the appetite for food and drink, to sustain our health, and the God-given gift of passion for pleasure, in which procreation of life is assured. In our FREE WORLD money and power are the measure and motivation of our actions.

Each of these gifts, used positively, can enhance and empower our lives. Likewise, used negatively, the abuse of these gifts can bring about negative consequences. This truth is the application of the natural law of "CONSEQUENCES."

Nothing I write in this Preface is new, rather it is presented in a way to help us understand the truth about life and existence—the truth about choices and consequences that Chuck writes about as his story unfolds in the pages that follow. The thoughts expressed in this Preface are not written to impress, rather they are written to encourage everyone to think about who we are and the power we have to define our future through our choices.

My effort to communicate and educate is not an ego trip, rather it is a response to the request of Chuck Gallagher, author of this book, to share my insights into his life. Chuck and I came together some years ago when, through my firm, he was offered a SECOND CHANCE. Now, as years have passed, Chuck expresses through this work, a desire to share his life story with others, in hopes that it will help someone else avoid the temptation he experienced—namely, the consequences of his misuse of our God-given "FREE WILL."

"DISCIPLINE" has always been the key word in my life that has led to all success and happiness and that I have been taught and privileged to understand from my many mentors. I have become the benefactor of this knowledge for which I give thanks daily, and remind myself that I am always accountable to a higher source and power than any of us can conceive. We all must answer for our greatest gift of "FREE WILL." So be it!

I wish to thank Chuck for motivating me to write these thoughts, and I will end by expressing my appreciation for Chuck openly sharing his real life story and thereby helping others learn from his own mistakes and experiences. Chuck paid a bitter penalty for his transgressions. Yet, his subsequent choices offered him an opportunity to be forgiven and receive a "Second Chance" —an opportunity to turn adversity into opportunity.

As I pen these words, we, too, must realize that none of us are perfect. We all learn from experience and ask forgiveness on our own for those issues in which we did not use good judgment or discipline. Each day we have the opportunity, through "FREE WILL," to make choices that empower us to become the spiritual beings that we were created to be. I am thankful to have played a part in Chuck's life and know that those who read the following pages will be touched.

One thing is a fact, the natural sacred law of "consequences" does prevail! Make your choices wisely so that the law of "consequences" can provide you "SECOND CHANCES" and positive results.

—Frank Stewart
Chairman of the Board
Stewart Enterprises
New Orleans, LA

Acknowledgments

We Aren't in This Alone

---◆---

As I look back at the more than twelve years since I began writing this book, I have come to understand that life is a journey, taken with many players—some playing a small role and others featured as stars. To those who have crossed my path but are not mentioned here, let me say "thank you." The words you uttered in kindness, or those that seemed harsh, were for my benefit, although at the time I may not have thought so. I know better now.

First, without the help of my friend Mary Auda and the outstanding team Milli Brown at Brown Books has assembled, this book would not have come into reality. Mary has been a contributing writer, helping me tap into the emotion associated with my experience. Her insight and the connection that we have make it easy to work together. Thanks to all at Brown Books for their leadership and guidance. Thanks also to Word Music Group, Inc., for permission to use the lyrics of "Trust His Heart."

Robert "Buck" Arrington, you befriended me, took care of me, taught me, and inspired me. I would never have thought my cellmate in prison would have had such an impact, but each time I deliver my presentation, I mention you, and through that, I thank you. You made my incarceration bearable and converted what could have been a nightmare into a powerful learning experience.

The following people I can never repay, but each of you saw value in the person "Chuck Gallagher," when I obviously didn't see value in myself. To Lynn Nichols, Jerry Stephens, Donald Smith, Brightsie Stroud, Doris Abee, Mary Annie Abee, and Drucilla Gallagher—I thank you for helping me. In life it is difficult to repay a debt of kindness. I hope that through my speaking and writing I can help others, and that by doing so I will be paying the debt I owe each of you. Paying it forward is powerful and because of your help and guidance I am afforded that opportunity.

To my ex-wife and the wonderful mother of my children—JeanA'—I am truly sorry for the pain I caused you. I know that your life is different because of the choices I made. However, I am thankful that we came together in love and that the product of that love has been our two sons, Rob and Alex. Your kindness allowed me to have the opportunity to become a father—something I went without during my childhood. I may not have been a great father by many standards, but I have done the best I know how, considering the circumstances.

To my two sons: you are the reason I am here. When all was lost in prison and I felt there was nothing to live for, I thought of you. I am proud of the men you have become. I'm sure that looking back, you may have wanted a different dad. But one thing I know for sure is that you could never find a dad who loves you more. Thank you for being who you are, and know that you have the power to overcome any obstacle placed before you; that's in your genes.

Lastly, to my loving wife, Deb. I don't know where to start. You have been there as a support and a sounding board. You've offered a kind touch when needed and moved me in the direction of my dreams. I know there are times that my weaknesses have been a bit much to bear, yet you have been there with me knowing that this is a spiritual journey. Thank you for your love, for being there, and for your support in the journey thus far. I look forward to the journey continuing.

1

The End Is the Beginning

---◆---

On the day I took twenty-three steps into prison, I did not recognize all the choices that resulted in this consequence. By the time I took twenty-three steps out of prison, my understanding had deepened. Writing this book led me to twenty-three insights about turning negative choices into positive results. I offer my story to remind you, and me, that our prisons are often self-inflicted.

All my efforts and actions had led to this point. What should have been fifteen years of solid success was nothing of the kind. Rather, I was about to be marked with a distinction I would likely carry for the rest of my life. It was the continuation of a learning process that would have profoundly positive benefits, but I couldn't see them right then. At the moment the alarm rang that early October morning, I could think of very little other than what was going to happen in just a few short hours.

I had packed the night before for this journey. What I was allowed to take was meaningless—mostly the clothes on my back. By that time, I really didn't have anything. The car I normally drove belonged to the company, so I turned it in as I resigned from my job. I had no other choice. I was now unemployed and had no clue what opportunity for employment I would find after I completed the next phase of my life.

My marriage was shot. We had been separated for several years with little hope of reconciliation. I guess there is a time when both parties know that it's over, even if they don't say so. Fortunately, my children still loved their daddy. My path was clouded in mystery for me and for my kids. That caused me concern because I didn't know how they would deal with it.

I owned no home, and what few possessions I had were meager and without value. Going from wealth to its utter opposite was never something I anticipated. At this stage of life, possessions were of little consequence. For so long in my life, my identity was defined by my career. Now I had no career, and my identity—well, I had no idea.

I recall my last weekend, which was spent with my children, being as normal as possible. I wanted to milk every last moment from that time. My mission was to be near them, to touch them, to let them know they were loved. They knew me as one person, and I was getting ready to be another. They seemed to have a good time during our last weekend together. Even though we had a great time, when I looked into their eyes I could tell they were concerned. They didn't know what to expect either and weren't even sure what to ask me in order to make them feel better. All I could remember was the love I saw in their eyes as I said good-bye that weekend and the sadness I felt as I drove away.

My best friend in the world was scurrying around that morning, trying to get ready. She was to take me on this new journey and, if there was any day that being late was not an option, today was one of those days. Still, I felt like dragging my feet. Up to this point, for the most part, I had always felt in control, always able to direct my destiny. Willing my fate had seemed natural. Well, I had manifested a destiny, all right, just not the one that I consciously had wanted.

"Are you ready to go?" she asked.

I wanted to answer, "No, but what choice do I have?" Instead, I said, "Sure." She gave me a hug, one that I wished would have lasted forever, and we proceeded out into the chill of the morning. She drove. I could have—in fact, she offered to let me—but I needed the time to reflect, to enjoy the beauty of my surroundings one last time. Besides, she tended to drive slower, and I was in no rush to get to my destination. Even ten years later, I can remember that morning vividly and how I was thinking, *slow down!*

We didn't talk much that morning. Being a garrulous person, I tend to chatter a bit, but not this day. I think I was caught in an emotional abyss. I didn't know what to feel. Normally confident and focused, that day I was unsure of who I was and what lay ahead. I seemed to have lost my identity, and that feeling was uncomfortable, if not downright scary. Sometimes in life we face life-changing events. This was certainly going to be one. The only question was what kind of outcome lay ahead.

I remember being taught that most folks live in either the past, the present, or the future. Well, I lived in the future. However, that day was pulling me out of the future, out of the realm I most liked to live in. I had no future. As I looked forward, all I saw was darkness. Although I knew, intellectually, that time brought me to this point and soon time would take me from it, I felt as if time were standing still and nothing lay ahead but darkness. The past had brought me to this point, and the present was uncertain and scary. All of this I had brought on myself. I forced myself to think that, perhaps on a higher level, there was some benefit. Whatever that might be seemed to be lost in the moment.

The closer we got to my destination, the more my throat tightened and my chest felt heavy. Traveling through the country, I wished the road would go on forever. Passing more and more civilization caused me to know that my time was near. We take for granted the freedom we enjoy—the freedom to live our lives and make so many choices. It doesn't even register until we face losing it; then, it becomes precious. I didn't realize how precious at that point.

As we pulled into the entrance gate, I reached to hand my papers to the man in uniform. With a certain look of disdain, he glanced my way and gave my companion clear and distinct instructions where to go. We pulled away slowly and yet, far too quickly, we arrived at my final destination.

As I opened the passenger door, time seemed to change. Everything was in slow motion, as if to etch this experience in my memory. I took my first steps into this new life. Visions of my family filled my heart and mind. They seemed lost to me. I took more steps, with thoughts of my ruined career. Yet more steps, with a strong sense that I literally had nothing.

On the twenty-third step, I extended my hand, opened the door, and took my first step into federal prison. As I walked toward the entrance, I was "Chuck Gallagher"—a person, some from my community would have, at one time, called a "somebody." As I walked through the door, I became 11642.058—a convicted felon—a person most people would call a "nobody."

We all have many rivers to cross as we journey through life, but this one left me wondering how I would ever find my way back to who I was and who I would become. For me this was bottom—rock bottom. By stripping away, in a very public way, an identity founded on ego, pride, and illusion, I was embarking on a new experience with an uncertain outcome.

> That twenty-third step propelling me into
> federal prison was proof positive to me that there is a
> consequence for every action.

I would never in my wildest dreams have conceived that in five short years I could so completely destroy my life. As a Tax Principal in a CPA firm in the mid-eighties, I exuded success. I had been published in national tax publications, testified before the United States House Ways and Means Committee on tax legislation, and become an instructor to CPAs in thirty states.

In some ways, the success seemed to come easily. Not that it didn't require work, but work was not an issue for me. Having been reared poor by most standards, I was taught at an early age that anything worth having was worth working toward. Had I been showered with my desires, I would not have been the person that I became. My rearing taught me the value of work and accomplishment. What I was fortunate to accomplish in my career came with hard work and a desire to succeed.

My father died when I was two years old. As a young child being reared by my mother, I vividly recall her telling me, "Son, don't ever let your circumstances hold you back. You can be 'somebody!'" I always remembered her words, but I find myself wondering how we ever survived on my mother's meager income. Somehow, we did, and I never recall going without anything of substance. My mother always seemed to be able to manifest what we needed just in time.

My mother's heart was pure, and her love for me was deep. Little did she know, and certainly I had no clue, that the statement or affirmation she spoke to me would have a profound effect in the future. "You can be somebody!" A powerful statement—but at depth, it implied that I was nobody. Looking back, I have come to understand that all my life I was chasing the elusive "somebody" to become and missed the fact that I was already somebody. Choices and consequences made that clear later in life.

Looking back, I see one thing crystal-clear, what being "somebody" means. One thing that we all learned in the college of business was the power of leverage. For example, we learned quickly that if you buy the biggest house you can barely afford, two fundamental things should happen: your income will increase and the value of your home should increase. Therefore, as your equity increases, so does your power to use leverage to buy more. Some call this the American dream. I now see it as a potential recipe for disaster.

As a quick learner, I understood the power of leverage to gain greater physical possessions. I also found that successful people wanted to be surrounded by other successful people, and that the measure of success is often gauged by surface appearance and possessions. Your dress, your automobile, your home and its location were all measures of success and value. And make no mistake; I wanted to be on that fast track to success.

Not long after the birth of my first child, I received a call from my local banker asking if there was a problem. Their records showed that I was behind in my house payment—not one month, but two! The truth was that I was behind. In fact, I was what some would call overextended and underfunded. In other words, I couldn't comfortably pay my bills, and what was worse, the financial community was starting to realize that. What a disaster for someone who made his living helping others with their money.

During our lives, we will all be faced with temptation many times. How we respond to temptation determines the measure of a man. I did not respond well. Through a series of choices, I set into motion the outcome that I took twenty-three steps to experience.

I committed fraud. I stole money. I had a need. I had to make the house payment or risk losing favor in the financial community. As a trustee of a client, I had an opportunity to divert funds without anyone being immediately aware. I could rationalize my action by calling my theft a "loan." My response to temptation was theft.

Of course, at the time I didn't call it theft. On the contrary, by paying back the "loan" with interest, I rationalized that not only was it a loan, but it was a new and valuable source of financing. I could further perpetuate the successful illusion I was so carefully creating. I took more.

I lived at that time in what seemed a parallel universe. I was making choices that brought about legitimate success. Yet, at the same time, I lived this shadow existence, making choices that ultimately brought about my downfall. Every choice generates consequences. The outcomes of the choices we make can be extraordinarily positive or extremely negative. The one fact we must all live by is that we will reap what we sow. The consequences of our choices may not manifest immediately, but we will harvest the outcome of our choices and actions. That twenty-third step propelling me into federal prison was proof positive to me that there is a consequence for every action. My own actions got me there.

This book is not about white-collar crime, theft, or lying, though I was guilty of all of them. More important than the crime are the prisons we can find ourselves in, most created by our own actions. The real challenge is how we escape those chains that bind us. How do we move past negative behaviors and create an environment that reflects true success?

When I was forced to admit my crimes, some four years after they began, that started a new and very different chapter in my life—one that I am living today. That chapter didn't unfold to success immediately. Rather, the process of change was long and arduous. I was blessed with many teachers, most of whom cut me no slack, but all of whom saw more humanity and value in me than I obviously saw in myself.

One of my first teachers was a businessman in my community who gave me my first job after my career as a CPA had been destroyed by my self-inflicted sabotage. To this day, I am not sure why he took the risk. On a spiritual level, I believe that everything happens for a reason. He accepted the role of mentor, teacher, and earthly angel. He believed in me when few around me would.

There were no handouts. He cut me no slack. Quite the contrary: this angel was tough. In fact, I'd say he was the toughest person for whom I ever worked. Yet he and two other mentors, along with my family, allowed me to make full restitution to those from whom I had stolen money. The act of honestly admitting what I had done and accepting the consequences of those actions was critical to making any worthwhile changes. While paying people back was significant, it didn't change what I had done and the pain I had caused. Those scars are permanent.

Time in prison seemed to move in slow motion, as if to allow me all the time necessary to evaluate my actions, my choices, and my behavior—and learn. If I had to be there, surely there should be an outcome worth the time. While I didn't know what that outcome would be, one thing I was committed to was remaining open to believing that God's plan for my life could rise from even this lowly place, if only I were willing to learn, grow, and receive.

> The act of honestly admitting what I had done and accepting the consequences of those actions was critical to making any worthwhile changes.

Eleven months after I entered prison, I took twenty-three steps out. Leaving the confines of regular prison to enter a halfway house was a profound first step. The awe of being placed back into mainstream society, even if that meant finishing my sentence in a halfway house, was inspiring. The loss of freedom, the loss of contact, and the isolation that comes from being incarcerated are significant. Those first steps brought a heartfelt joy.

In order to transition to a halfway house, I had to have a job. Because of the seeds I had planted with my former employer, from 1991 onward, I was fortunate to be considered for reemployment. I was given the opportunity to make a living in sales on straight commission. What I did with that opportunity was directly a result of the choices I made.

Each inmate was required to notify the halfway house of their location and of every movement made during the day. I was happy to comply. The opportunity to rebuild my life was far too precious. No mistakes or bad choices could be tolerated. My past choices had not served me well, so this new opportunity gave me a chance to change the course of my life.

Within eight months, after taking the same twenty-three steps out of that prison door, I was recognized for the choices I had made and offered the chance to take a management role. I had no expectations that this would happen but accepted, with gratitude, the opportunity placed before me.

As spiritual beings, whether we like to admit it or not, we create our reality. The multitude of choices made each day, following my release from prison, created the opportunity I was to receive. My abundance and prosperity continued to multiply. Within three months of my reentry into management, I was presented with another promotion—sales management supervisor of two states.

Never in my wildest dreams could I have predicted that one year from my prison release date, I would be managing a $6 million sales organization. A clear pattern was beginning to emerge. Choices made with integrity provided positive consequences. I was living proof of both sides of the choice issue. Choices made without integrity or ethics certainly yielded extraordinary negative consequences. Those choices made from an ethical framework, with a foundation of integrity, were yielding results far beyond my expectations.

The road to recovery is not easy. Soon after I took my new job in sales, the area I was working in was ravaged by a powerful hurricane. Unless I was selling generators or roofing repair, no one wanted to buy a product while they focused on rebuilding their lives following a catastrophic event.

Was I a victim of nature's wrath? How can I expect to succeed when there is devastation all around me? These were good questions—just not the right questions. Life is not about luck. It's about choices! I could have deviated from the path and experienced a less-than-certain outcome. Or, I could've done exactly what I chose and stayed focused on daily making the right choices that would pave a path to eventual recovery and prosperity.

Can we change our lives? Yes! We are given the creative power to manifest our present and our future, just as we have created our past. I wish I had gotten this concept much earlier in life. Perhaps I could have been spared the pain associated with time in prison. We all face our prisons, and they are mostly self-inflicted.

I took twenty-three steps and learned life is not about the prisons we find ourselves in; it's about breaking the chains that bind us so we can achieve growth, insight, and success beyond measure.

2

Mirror, Mirror, on the Wall

———————— ◆ ————————

Stunned silence. That's what I recall, in those first few seconds when I heard the voice of my business partner. In an instant, I knew my life would never be the same. The next few seconds were a blur as I tried to clear my mind and formulate my response.

"Chuck? Did you hear what I said?" my partner asked.

Just moments ago, I was in "the flow" as I taught a class in Boise, Idaho; it was going great. The participants were responding, getting their credits, and having a good time as well. I could tell that another good evaluation was forthcoming, and that I'd be asked to teach more classes. There was nothing quite like speaking to twenty, two hundred, or two thousand people. I loved teaching, and students loved me. I felt on top of the world.

As we broke for lunch, I noticed a message slip on the door for me. I usually did not get a message to call back to my office. Most of the time I knew that in my absence they had everything under control. I wasn't concerned about the call; my only dilemma was when to call. Considering the different time zones, if I waited to call back after class the office would be closed. So my decision was to take some of my lunch break and return the call.

Not expecting the call to be significant or to take long, I moved away from the noise of the lunch area and placed the call. I was stunned by what I heard. "Chuck, one of your clients called earlier today and said you had helped him invest some money. His circumstances have changed, and he needs to liquidate that investment immediately. I know you will not be back until Friday, so tell me where the file is, and I'll get the process started."

Most of the time, I am not at a loss for words. I felt the room spin and held on to the wall. In the entirety of the universe, there were only two entities who knew the truth—God and I. As I heard those words, I knew my life would change forever and that the truth would be known by many. My earlier elation about the success of the class quickly was gone, and I saw my life pass in front of me as if I were dying.

"Did you hear what I said?" my partner asked.

I found my voice. "Yes. So sorry, Dan," I responded. "I was distracted by one of the class participants. We just broke for lunch."

"Well, you get on to your class. Just tell me what to do and where the file is, and I'll help get the liquidation started. He seemed real antsy about his money."

What my partner did not know, what no one knew, was that I had not invested money for clients—I had stolen money from clients. There was nothing to liquidate, and there was no way I could create the kind of money my client needed in order to repay my theft. The theft I had perpetrated over the past several years and the illusion of grand success I created was rapidly crashing. I had no clue what to say. I could only buy time.

"Dan, you don't know where to begin. Let me make a few calls and get the process started. I'll be back in the office on Friday. Just give my client a call and let him know it's under control. Now, sorry, but I've got to get back to class." And with those words, the call ended. I had bought myself some time, but time for what?

No one in the class I was teaching knew what had just happened. The folks at my office had no clue what was going to happen. My client had no clue that the funds he needed weren't there. Most importantly, my family had no clue that their life was about to change radically.

The choices I had made were destined to have a dramatic effect on everyone I had touched. The time for the real consequences and drama to unfold was now.

The rest of the day was a blur. There is not one thing I remember about the afternoon session I was teaching. The participants were laughing, posing questions, and engaged. I don't remember even being there. I was hungry before I made the call at our lunch break, but after the call, I couldn't eat a thing. All I recall was a numb, spacey feeling. I was powerless. No longer was I in control. I had been on a merry-go-round for some time, and today—this day—the Universe said, "enough!" I was flung off, and I could tell that the landing was going to be hard.

As the class ended and the last participant made his exit, I sat in the empty hotel conference room drained, sick to my stomach, not knowing what to do or what steps to take. I can't say my life had been without challenges. In most cases, I rose to the occasion and met them head on. This time, though, was different. My choices had made my life unmanageable. There was nowhere to turn that would solve the mess I had created. I was good at creating the illusions, but I could think of nothing that would allow me to escape the fate which I was coming to realize I must face. Nothing!

> I was good at creating the illusions, but I
> could think of nothing that would allow me to escape the fate
> which I was coming to realize I must face.

Until that point, I had dismissed people who had expressed feelings of despair or depression as weak. As egotistical as it sounds, I felt that those of keen mind could always be in control of themselves and their emotions. And, I felt I was one of those—no depression for me.

Since then, I've come to understand the feelings that certainly can come from personal feelings of powerlessness. As smart as I thought I was, I was not smart enough to avoid universal laws and their application.

Every choice has a consequence, and I was quickly becoming aware that I had no power over the consequences that were about to unfold. All I could do for the moment was sit like a whipped pup in an empty conference room and cry—hoping that the maintenance staff would stay away long enough for me to compose myself.

As I collected my thoughts that fateful day and reluctantly went to my room in the hotel for the evening, I knew one thing for certain—the choices that brought a temporary illusion of joy were causing me to look squarely in the mirror. And I didn't like what I saw. There was no joy in my eyes that night. I saw only the pain my decisions were about to cause those I loved and who loved me.

Physical pain is just not something that I'm good with. I have often said that I'm allergic to needles, as I can't stand the pain of a simple shot or bee sting. Yet, that night I contemplated suicide.

Desperation soon set in as I lay in my hotel bed contemplating the trip back home the next morning. What would I say to my business partners? What would I say to my wife? What lay ahead for my life? With two young children at home, what would happen if my wife left with the children and I never saw them again?

I was at a breaking point, feeling that I had no control and no value. In my current state, I was useless to my partners; in fact, I was a severe detriment. Everything my wife and I had worked for was about to vanish; only she didn't know that. Furthermore, the career that I had worked so hard to craft was going to disintegrate in just a matter of hours. I had no control. I was powerless. The only rational action I could think of was ending my life.

Thank God for that major phobia of mine—fear of pain. The problem with suicide was that everything I thought of involved pain. I even considered jumping off the building, but the distance between the leap forward and the final impact caused me some serious worry. What would I be thinking during those few seconds? More importantly—"Good Lord, that would hurt!"

At 7:11 p.m. that evening, I grabbed the Yellow Pages and began calling clinics—anyone who I thought might help me. Frankly, I don't recall what I was looking up. I do remember that there were no listings under "suicide"—in fact, that wasn't a category. So I looked up physicians, psychologists, psychiatrists, anything that started with a "P". Honestly, I don't remember who I did call—a proctologist, as far as I knew. The only thing that flooded my mind was I needed help.

"You've reached the office of Drs . . . Our office hours are from 8:30 a.m. to 5:00 p.m. Our office is closed. But if you'll leave your name and number, we'll be happy to call you first thing in the morning. Have a nice day!" Somehow, when you're thinking of ending your life, "have a nice day" just doesn't seem appropriate. And unfortunately, that's the message I got over and over.

Calling became an obsession. It was the one thing I could do, one action that I felt in life I had some control over. "Just one more dial," I would say to myself as I pressed the buttons on the phone, listening to the ring, hoping for an answer.

"Dr. Benson's office." That was the second time that day I was stunned. After getting recording after recording, I was somewhat unprepared for the possibility that someone would answer. Yet someone did.

"I need to talk with someone. I'm from out of town," I somehow stammered.

"Actually, our office is closed. I was just walking out the door and thought this was my wife. Give us a call in the morni . . . "

Before he could finish his sentence, I blurted, "I'm thinking of committing suicide!"

Silence—then the voice said, "Let's talk."

For the life of me, I can't recall what was said between us as I lay on that lonely hotel bed. We could have talked for two minutes, twenty minutes, or two hours. I just don't remember. What I do recall is that this total stranger, a man who I had never met, took the time

15

to help me see past the grand illusion I had created and uncover the real me inside.

That night was the darkest night of my soul. That call that I shared didn't make it better. It didn't eliminate the consequences. It didn't remove the pain. Rather, it gave me hope, hope that if I could make poor choices that would, most certainly, bring painful consequences, I also possessed the power to make positive choices with positive results.

His comment to me still resounds in my heart today. He said, "You have made a terrible mistake, but YOU are not a mistake! The choices you make moving forward will define your life forever and provide the foundation for your children's lives. Think carefully as you make this choice!"

When he said to me, "YOU are not a mistake," it hit me—while the past cannot be changed, the life we are given and the choices we make moving forward are the only things that count. I felt a burden lifted. I could not change the past; all I could do was face the consequences. It was within my power to make good choices, now and in the future, that would produce a fruitful outcome. That was my destiny!

In the years since that fateful night, time after time, I have wondered who I talked with that dismal evening. I'm quite certain that on that morning so many years ago, this individual didn't get up, prepare for work, kiss his wife goodbye, and leave, saying, "I'm gonna save a life today!" No; rather, I suspect that it was a normal day for him, just like it started out being a normal day for me. But for us both, that day ended on a profound note. I just wish I could say thank you!

Perhaps the best way to repay my debt to a man who took time away from his family to save mine is to pay it forward. How many times have people unexpectedly come into our lives and had an unexpected impact? Perhaps we may experience a kind comment or someone taking the time to listen when we needed to be heard? Paying it forward, however, means we need to be that person to someone else. Are we prepared to stop and listen? Are we willing to help others when they need our support? Can we listen unconditionally? Is it possible that we might be called upon one day when we least expect it, just like my angel that night?

Looking back, it was a pivotal moment when there was no escaping the choices I had made and the consequences that, in my heart, I surely knew would follow. This was that moment for me, but what about for you? Time and time again, as I share this story with others, I find people approaching and telling me their defining moment. We all, at some point in our lives, find ourselves imprisoned by our own choices. The question remains: what prison are you in?

Some choices seem so small and insignificant at the time that we hardly even notice them. Often, the choices we make define the prison we find ourselves in and the drama that plays out in our lives. The first time you make the choice to smoke cigarettes seems irrelevant until the last years of your life when you might find your body racked with emphysema or you are dying of lung cancer. That first drink of alcohol rarely is considered significant. To some, it never is. Yet to many, the consequences of alcohol are debilitating and destructive. They can lead to consequences that are life changing for all who are connected. Perhaps you come from a loving and close-knit family. Then a parent dies and harsh words are spoken as funeral and estate decisions have to be made. The family splits, and years later you find yourself longing for the relationship you once had.

> Often the choices we make define the prison we find ourselves in and the drama that plays out in our lives.

Every choice has a consequence. The mystery behind choices and consequences is that we often don't realize the magnitude of what we do until it's too late. Then, we often wish we could rewind the tape and choose something different. As my partner spoke those words on the phone, I wished I had made different choices, because the consequences of my actions would be enormous.

A friend of mine recently asked me if I would consider mentoring a young man, twenty-three years old, who was in prison as a result of his choices. She explained that when he was twenty years old, he was out with his buddies drinking, and he was the designated driver. He elected to drink. Perhaps not at the rate of his friends, but he drank. He was underage.

When they left the bar, he was tossed the keys by his plastered friend. The drunk buddy began prodding the driver to pass "that slow car" in front of them. Not wanting to bring attention to them, the driver followed slowly for a while. Meanwhile, the prodding persisted until the "designated driver" could take no more. With a quick jerk, he maneuvered the truck into the opposite lane to pass. Control was lost. The truck flipped. His buddy was thrown from the vehicle, and the vehicle landed on his body. Manslaughter was the verdict.

Days later, the parents and loved ones of the man killed in this tragic accident played out what is seen daily in cemeteries across the nation—the burial of a life tragically lost. The driver was devastated at the death of his friend, not to mention his ten-year sentence. The parents and loved ones of the driver will be reminded forever of the choice made that fateful night that wrought a tragic consequence.

The consequence was quick and certain. That doesn't always happen. In fact, many may be lulled into the false belief that there is no consequence if they don't see one quickly. How dangerous! We cannot escape the consequences of our actions and choices. No matter how hard we try, there is always a consequence—that is a universal law.

In the past, I was very judgmental about people and their lives. I was arrogant in my judgment. Although a part of me still carries some of that today, I have learned compassion. The situations we find ourselves in are often created by our own choices. One lady I recently talked with said, rather indignantly, "Surely you don't think that somehow I was responsible for that, do you?" At the risk of alienating some who read this book, I must say, "Yes." I think by our choices we create our lives, our outcomes, our consequences, whether good or bad. We create them.

I understand that we are all spiritual beings having human experiences. While every choice has a consequence and some aren't so pleasant, those who suffer dreaded outcomes still feel pain. As humans, we can feel compassion, even though often the outcome and pain may be justified. Many of us learn our lessons best through hitting rock bottom and experiencing the pain that accompanies the consequences that follow.

Ask yourself honestly: what in your life would you truly like to change? Would you like your relationship with your spouse, children, or parents to be better? If you could, would you undo some choice, hidden though it might be, that you made in the past? Would you change your eating habits, stop smoking, or stop drinking? What would you do that, if done correctly, would bring you true joy?

Mirror, mirror, on the wall. Sometimes looking in the mirror forces us to look past the illusions we've created to the reality hidden beneath our well-crafted surface. Maybe just then we can grasp the reality of how to begin to loosen those chains that bind us to the prisons we've created and come to enjoy the blessings of true freedom.

The fact that we might have avoided the consequence only plays to the illusion that there isn't one. However, illusions are funny things; they appear real. We can trick our conscious mind into believing that the illusion we see or we live is reality. Yet, in the end, we cannot escape the outcomes from the choices we make. In the end, when we look in the mirror, the one person who is always there when the drama unfolds is the person who made the choice. In my case, that was me!

3

Help . . . I Need Somebody

My partner's cold, steel-blue eyes seemed to stare right through me as if I weren't there. There were no words spoken between us. Just silence broken only by the sound of him tapping his pencil in nervous tension—or was it anger?

Meanwhile, the chatter of "what-if's" became noise in my head that had not ceased since I sought sleep the night before in Boise. That night had been a life or death decision for me. I chose to live and deal with the consequences. Even though that was my wish, the endless chatter within my head was telling me otherwise, and it was confusing. Everything seemed daunting, and I felt so overwhelmed. I could find no solutions. There was no rest.

I played what I would say to them over and over again in my mind as I traveled across the continent back home. Debating with whom to talk to first, I concluded that talking to my partners would be easier than talking to my wife. Frankly, the last thing I wanted to do was talk to my wife, knowing that, as the words streamed from my mouth, it would literally shatter her world. Although built on illusion, our world was her security—something she could rely on and be proud of. Never in her wildest dreams would she think that in one instant, everything would change. I could only guess what her response would be. How I dreaded that conversation.

I looked up at my partners, wishing they would say something—anything. I wondered if I should speak, but their faces signaled clearly that this was a time of silence for me.

Perhaps, just perhaps, they would be more understanding considering the successful business we built together. I slipped into denial again. Creating illusions was second nature for me. Perhaps they would help me find a solution. After all, my choices would have a direct effect on their livelihood in the CPA practice. Maybe, just maybe, we could devise a way to cover it all up, make restitution, and move on. Maybe that would be best for us all. Then, out of the silence, my partner said, "Well, I have a solution!"

I couldn't believe my ears. For the first time in almost twenty-four hours, I felt that perhaps someone with a clearer head than mine could make some sense of this mess I created. With a small feeling of hope, I looked up into my partner's eyes. I wasn't going to have to go through this alone. There was a way out. I don't know what he saw, sitting across the table from me. I felt a gleam in my eye, anticipating some solution, any solution, that would ease this burden.

"I think you should kill yourself!" There was no emotion in his voice. As I stared into his eyes, I realized that he was dead serious.

"Your debts would be paid. After all, you've had life insurance long enough that there should be no suicide clause. The community would take pity on your children and rally around your wife and save her from the shame of your actions. Chuck, frankly, you don't deserve to live."

Only moments before, I had a brief glimpse of hope only to be crushed by the words of my partner. I had committed to maintain control of my emotions, but at that moment, reality set in. There wasn't going to be an easy way out. My choices were destined to have consequences; the first was disconnection from my partners.

"Chuck, you're fired." My other partner spoke without emotion, but perhaps with a little compassion. "We can't keep you on here. I'm sure you understand that. However, killing yourself isn't an option either.

Your children deserve more than that. Now, let's get on with the next steps; you owe us that."

I knew he was right. I felt sick as I realized that my selfish choices were about to unleash a plethora of unwanted consequences on so many people, including my family. What was the right thing to do when I had done so much wrong? The question was clear, the answer even clearer: make the right choices! My life depended on it.

For the next hour and a half, I shared with my partners the details of the frauds I had committed. They were shocked at times, mostly overwhelmed, and clearly concerned about the consequences that my actions would cause them. My choices not only impacted my family but also their families. They had children to put through school and had a thriving business—at least, they thought it was thriving until that day. They had the respect of the community. Now what would happen to them? I put my head into my hands and shook my head in disbelief. What had I done? How did I get here?

As they tried to make sense of everything, they would ask questions. "What did you do with all that money?" one of my partners asked. I was being peppered with questions like bullets from an automatic weapon. "Do you have a problem with drugs or gambling? I mean, how can you have nothing to show for a quarter of a million dollars?"

The questions kept coming, one right after the other. When a crisis arises, usually human nature tries to make sense of it. As they grasped the enormity of my theft, control was what they needed. As I would later discover, these questions were just a taste of what was to come. We'd talk details for a while until it became overwhelming, and then the questions would begin again. Looking back, I can't really imagine how they must have felt. Betrayed? Shocked? Bewildered? What did they do to deserve their lives being so drastically changed?

I did not expect rejection from my partners, at least not as quickly and cleanly as it happened. Somehow I lived under the deluded, misguided attitude that perhaps, in order to cover up my incredible misdeeds, my partners and I might figure out a way to make restitution and move on. That would have put a Band-Aid on the problem. The lessons would have been short-lived. If that had happened, the only result would have been more bad choices, creating yet even greater negative outcomes.

> ## Success, greed, and power kept me oblivious to the inevitable outcome I was beginning to face.

Yet part of me wanted that solution—just to clean up the mess and continue as if nothing had changed. As those thoughts went through my head, I knew that my life had become unmanageable. What seemed to be the perfect illusion had become an insatiable nightmare. The money went to lifestyle. The lifestyle created the illusion, which demanded more money. I was no more in control than a plane flying without a pilot. Being blinded by success, greed, and power kept me oblivious to the inevitable outcome I was beginning to face.

As long as I could manage the illusion, juggle the theft, and move forward with life as I knew it, I was fine. During that time, never once did I come to believe that I could not pay back and move on undetected. I felt an almost invincible attitude. I was smart, in control, and feeding my ego, never sensing that I had created a house of cards that had no chance of surviving intact. I had no conscious idea that all it would take was for one card to be removed and the house would tumble down. That card had been pulled two days before. I was standing in the middle of the crash with nowhere to turn, beginning to understand how little control I had in my life.

Because my wife was expecting her husband and the father of her two children to return later in the afternoon, I had time after meeting with my partners to call on my attorney. More than once, I've had people ask if my attorney was more important than my wife. Of course

24

not, but as soon as I walked out of the office where I had served as tax partner, I knew the legal wheels of justice would be greased and the consequence process begun. I needed to seek legal counsel and have a legal plan on which to move forward. I sought help from an attorney who was also a friend.

For once, our meeting wasn't about mutual clients or about how our family stories were unfolding—this time, I was the client. Not something he was expecting on a Friday midday, nor something he wanted. As I left the attorney's office, I could see the disappointment on his face. I didn't know that this would be the same look repeated many times over as friends and family discovered the truth of my illusion.

As I drove home, I realized I felt helpless. My power over the outcome had been reduced to zero. I couldn't control the players. I couldn't make the moves. I couldn't control the outcomes. The only thing I could do was focus moment by moment on the choices I was making and trust that a power greater than myself was in control. Since I had never been in this place before, I was moving blindly forward. I knew then that all I had left was a power greater than me.

The feeling of helplessness and not being in control was unfamiliar. Through luck, wit, or manipulation, there had always been a confidence that underpinned my decisions, a knowledge that I had the power to manipulate an outcome. Now that the manipulations no longer worked, and the reality of failure loomed, I realized that I never had "the power"—it was only an illusion, and I was a master illusionist.

In so many ways, we can control the outcome. Good choices yield good results. The law of reciprocity says you reap what you sow. Through personal experience, I have found that to be true. Yet, no matter the illusion, we can't change the forces of the universe. On Earth, denying gravity exists doesn't make it so. Once a choice is made, we can create an illusion of no consequence and deny its existence, but that doesn't make it so. Ultimately, we are responsible for our choices and the consequences that follow.

What is true is that we may not know what specifically the consequence is or how it will unfold. Often we might find that the outcome is far different from what we might have predicted or that the outcome takes unexpected twists and turns. But there is always an outcome, a consequence for every action.

Having told my story three times in detail—once to a counselor the night before in Boise, attempting to avoid suicide; again, to my now-former partners; and finally, to my attorney—didn't make the drive home any easier. This was going to be the most difficult and the most painful. What was I going to say? Admitting to the person I loved most in the world that I was a liar and a thief didn't seem natural. I felt I would lose everything I held most dear—the love of my wife and adoration of my children.

Pulling into the drive, I stopped short of the garage. I didn't want to alert anyone to my presence quite yet. I needed a moment to gather myself and prepare for the inevitable. I knew as I walked through the door that my oldest son would descend upon me, jumping into my arms, welcoming his daddy home. How I longed to see him and my youngest son, eight months old. My bonds with both of them had been set. I had been active with both of them as infants, feeding them in the wee hours of the morning, attending to their needs. Although I traveled frequently, they both thoroughly enjoyed the homecomings. When I was home, they showered me with unconditional love in a way that only children seem to do. This time, I just wanted to bathe in that love.

As I imagined the reunion with my children, I also sensed impending doom. This homecoming would certainly be a time of intense joy, and at the same time it would be filled with intense grief as I revealed the truth. After the meeting with my partners and their rejection, I knew that I would experience even greater rejection in what used to be the sanctity of my home. I was at the bottom. I knew that was the only place I could strip away the illusions and see the reality of who I was. Today I know what I didn't know then: my rock bottom was a gift of life. At that moment, it didn't feel like a gift. It felt like hell.

> Today I know what I didn't know then:
> my rock bottom was a gift of life.

As I closed the car door, I took a deep breath as I mustered the courage to keep a cheery face for my children, knowing that soon I'd be telling this story one more time and the person hearing it would be shocked. I knew when I walked through that door that not only my life would be changed but also the lives of my family. As the key slid into the door, my entry marked the beginning of yet more of the consequences.

I enjoyed our lifestyle. My wife enjoyed our lifestyle. Never once did it occur to her that the way we lived was built on an illusion. On that day, however, the truth was revealed. Ugly, unadulterated, bitter truth came pouring out to an unsuspecting recipient. She didn't ask for this. To her, all was unfair, unwanted, like living a waking bad dream. Through the tears and painful emotions, she just wanted it all to go away.

"Oh, God," she cried, "we need help!"

Somehow the cry for help came purely from her. Admitting my defects, hidden failures, character flaws, whatever one might call them, was not natural for me any more than seeking help. This time, she was right—there was no way we would ever make it through this without help.

This choice, uttered by two people crying, being consoled by a four-year-old who was struggling to make sense of this very odd homecoming, was the first right choice in a long while.

"We need help!"

4

The "Log" in Someone Else's Eye

You could almost hear the story spread as it sizzled across the phone lines. Little did I know that the next call I would receive would embroil me in a life lesson that I had neither awareness of nor inclination toward. I was on a collision course to learn, and as the phone rang in my office, the process began.

"You're not going to believe what I just heard," my wife said excitedly as she called me at work to spread the news. "You know our neighbor, Dr. Hoven?" A small town is always hot for a little gossip, and since it usually was about somebody's demise, it gave people something to feel pious about. I sighed as I prepared to hear the news.

"Yes. So what's the deal?" I asked.

"Well, Nancy called and said Beth told her that Dr. Hoven, just late last night, sexually molested the little Branson girl. You know, they live up the street. Can you believe that?" she said incredulously.

"Dr. Hoven?" I thought to myself. It didn't connect with the man I knew. "Come on, do you believe that?" I said to my wife. There was no way, knowing Dr. Hoven, that I would believe some fool gossip like that. I didn't mean to sound self-righteous, but having heard so many stories on folks that turned out not to be true, I was having a hard time fathoming this one. After all, what would cause a "successful," prominent doctor, happily married with children, to sexually molest a nine-year-old girl? It was so far out of my realm of experience that I just wasn't sure I believed it. The story was much too bizarre, and I was outraged at hearing it—not at him, but at the gossip mill.

Because we lived less than a block away, my wife was beside herself as the news spread like a vicious cancer over the phone lines. She swayed from being angry with the doctor and outraged by his actions to being concerned about the safety of her children. Many mothers throughout the community were reacting the same way.

For the better part of a week, the rumors swirled. People in the community were divided. Mothers were outraged at the possibility of such a vile action, while patients refused to believe a word of it. If the phone company had charged for each local call regarding the accusation, it would have made a fortune off of the conversations about the good doctor.

Choices made by the doctor just the night before were beginning to shape an outcome that would have far-reaching consequences. Just as those were taking shape, I was living a comfortable life—living an illusion while my shadow side stayed well hidden. My misdeeds were neatly tucked away, hidden from view for no one to know. After all, I had rationalized my actions and certainly could correct any choice I made. I wasn't a bad person, just a smart one, I thought. I knew how to beat the system. Feeling so invincible, I was soaring high; I believed that nothing could touch me. Little did I know.

While on Earth, we have a great opportunity for growth. Unfortunately, many of the lessons contained in experience are hidden from our conscious view within our subconscious mind. Because of the veil placed over humanity, most of us function with only a dim awareness of our purpose or mission. Life is our teacher, through which we receive many experiences. At some point, as we grow, the lessons show themselves. Then we can reflect on our experience and reap the consequences of our lessons.

I have come to understand that a situation that is less than joyful is there to teach us important lessons. We can learn from the lessons presented and gain insight and growth. That's our choice. To progress and learn, however, it is helpful to express our conscious intent to do so. The reality is that unless we recognize the lesson, events may continue unfolding until the lessons intensify. We must remain open to the teachings and gifts we are receiving in order to grow and evolve.

As we grow in our spiritual journey, we can progress to the point that we step out of our bodies and become conscious observers. At that point, we begin to sense that we're more in control of the situation than we imagined. By looking from the outside in, we can make a choice to respond in a way that serves our highest good. Self-awareness, in part, means that the veil has been partially lifted as we progress through our life lesson.

As I was watching the doctor's situation, I was learning myself. However, I didn't experience much self-awareness then. I was at the beginning of a long journey, which would take me spiraling downward into an opportunity for tremendous growth.

Weeks passed. Tongues wagged. All the while, the story of the doctor grew to enormous proportions. His actions were reprehensible, and enough damage had been done to cause dire consequences. Many of the townfolk were appalled.

> As I was watching the doctor's situation,
> I was learning myself. However, I didn't experience
> much self-awareness then.

As months passed, I witnessed the immense power of the tongue. Before ever determining guilt or innocence, the community tried him verbally; he was doomed by the very people he was there to serve. Some stood by him. They didn't condone his actions but wanted to support him spiritually as he and his family suffered. These people were also condemned.

Many of his patients sought medical care elsewhere. Battle lines were being drawn. Even casual association with the doctor drew criticism from others. By bringing harm to a child, he drew the wrath of the community, most of whom delighted in pointing fingers at the accused. It was a righteous cause, and people felt justified in participating in the finger-pointing. They were protecting the most helpless members of society, our children. Perhaps some of those were perpetrators of some crime, like me, and could feel self-righteous because their crime wasn't that bad compared to what he did. Pointing fingers at him removed the spotlight from me. Ironically, for every finger we point, three are pointing back. Somehow, then I didn't know that lesson. I could point my finger with the best of them.

The local newspaper delighted in publishing the bad news—albeit months later, after everyone in town already knew. The long arm of justice was about to be served. A plea bargain agreement was reached. Otherwise, the child victim would have to take the stand and relive the event over and over in public. She had suffered enough.

The doctor was sentenced to serve time in a work-release prison while all he had worked for crumbled around him. Shattered was the man many of us knew. He clearly was living the consequences of his actions as his child victim was, too. Lives were forever changed the night the doctor made sexual movements towards the child. It destroyed the illusion of safety in this small town and shook the very core of who people were. The changes reverberated through his family, his church, and his patients. The child would always be affected by the doctor's choice. No one was left unscathed.

From every direction, judgments poured in. Most were destructive; few seemed spiritual. His family stood with him, though. Looking back, I think that impressed me most. His action was reprehensible, but it created an opportunity for many people to learn and to grow. It tested the very foundation of faith within the community.

Now serving time in a kind of prison, Dr. Hoven would leave each day to work to support his family. His life was shattered. No longer did he garner any respect from the community. Everything he had worked for was gone. He was in financial ruin, doing his best to maintain some sense of dignity, knowing his responsibility to those he loved and let down by his actions. The judgments and criticisms were sharp and continued from the community. Perhaps these were his "just rewards"—an "eye for an eye."

In the Bible, it states, "Why do you see the speck that is in your brother's eye, but do not notice the log that is in your own eye? Or how can you say to your brother, 'Let me take that speck out of your eye,' when there is the log in your own eye? You hypocrite, first take the log out of your own eye, and then you will see clearly to take the speck out of your brother's eye" (Matthew 7:3–5). Dr. Hoven's situation showed me an example of spiritual truth that I had heard more than once. Yet, I was unwilling to heed its message—something I regret.

The last remnant the doctor retained of his former self was his medical license. Through all that he had been through—losing his job, suffering financially, and being criminally convicted—his medical license survived. The state medical licensing board was to hold a hearing regarding his license retention. Before the hearing, word leaked out in the community, and once again the self-appointed community advocates were up in arms.

First one neighbor called, then another. Word had it that the doctor's attorney wanted things kept quiet. With little publicity, his attorney indicated that the chance of keeping his medical license was pretty good. The likelihood of it being kept quiet was almost nil, especially in this close-knit community. The whole idea of this man again practicing medicine incensed some. Their mission was to rally community support to eliminate Dr. Hoven's medical license.

After all, with the crime he committed, why should he be given any opportunity to serve others and make a respectable income? They were on a mission, and they accomplished it with religious zeal.

"Would you write a letter to the medical board? I mean, do we really want this man to be in a position to abuse his power again? After all, he was caught doing this, but what else is there that we don't know about?" The call came in to me around midday from a female neighbor who seemed to be joyful about leading the rally. That barrage of questions represented only part of the phone conversations I had received. Calls initially went out from a small group. The plan was set in motion, and within twenty-four hours, that small group became a formidable opposition force. I was right there with the group. After all, how could I refuse? I was a pillar of the community and could lead the troops.

We have a tendency to mask or justify our own weakness by looking for or exploiting the weaknesses of others. Here I was, perpetuating a grand embezzlement scheme and yet attacking another for the "speck in his eye." I didn't see the reflection of myself in the mirror.

At this point, some might say, "Wait, your embezzlement, while bad, does not compare with a child's sexual abuse." Nevertheless, I violated the trust of my clients, my wife, my children, my partners, and my community. They experienced betrayal. Our prisons can be imposed or self-made. Often the self-made prisons provide far more punishment and are more difficult to leave. My attack on Dr. Hoven was from a position of being as guilty as he was. I had no business leading the "moral majority" against him. I recall a part of a conversation that I had with one of my neighbors. I said to him, "You know, if I took money from one of my clients, not only would I lose my license, but I would be put into jail."

Psychologically, I was attempting to rise above my own insufficiency. What we see in others often is a mirror of ourselves. What I clearly didn't see was that I was as guilty in my own way of illegal activities as was the doctor. On a spiritual level, if I had been able to get the beam out of my eye, I would have been able to see with spiritual clarity the divinity of my brother, the doctor. With him, I could have shared light and life and been an uplifting force in his life instead of being destructive. Likely, nothing would have changed for me and my outcome, but I would have the knowledge that I showed compassion rather than judgment.

The letter I wrote was a masterpiece. I made sure that all the areas of vulnerability were attacked. I wanted maximum effect. I knew the outcome I wanted, and I was controlling the circumstances to achieve that outcome. In a sense, this was a modern day crucifixion, and the letter I wrote hammered in the nails with expert precision. I had no idea of the karma I was creating for myself by this action.

There is always a different reality beyond every appearance. Although I was seeking to punish Dr. Hoven, my reality was punishing me. We are not punished for our sins, but rather, by them. In a sense, I feel that my actions helped create a similar outcome for me.

We are not punished for our sins,
but rather, by them.

We cannot break the law and go unpunished. At some point in our lives and in some way, our wrongdoings will come back to us. All mistakes, failures, or wrongdoings must somehow be atoned for at some time. Hindus call this "karmic debt." Such a concept is not limited to Hinduism. All religions incorporate this concept in some form or fashion. In the Bible, for example, there are statements that we reap what we sow. The real question is what that means for us.

Every mistake or failure will be atoned for. We choose whether we work out the cycle of retribution through prolonged suffering, or whether our debt repayment is satisfied through the discipline of rising above our current level of consciousness from which the act was committed to a higher spiritual understanding. As we speak, think, and act toward others, so shall we receive. What we do to others eventually comes back to us in some way.

Several in the community attended the medical hearing. They didn't speak. Rather, they allowed the letters sent by several of us to say all that needed to be said. Their presence at the hearing was merely a show of unity in favor of the doctor losing his license. The cards were stacked against Dr. Hoven the moment he walked through the door. His attorney made valiant arguments for his client, as he was paid to do. After all, he had never once had a complaint about his practice of medicine and, in fact, had helped many. Where were those people who would stand with him? Absent . . . at least, that day.

The judgment was rendered: Dr. Hoven's license was revoked. All the choices and sacrifices he had made, in less than a year, had all vanished due to an irrevocable choice he made one night. His choices affected many as they rippled through the community. He and his family were forced to leave the area. Some two decades later, I am not sure that the town knows where they are. The child he attempted to molest, now grown, surely has scars that have been hard to heal. People he served as a doctor have said they feel betrayed. Perhaps this incident was a catalyst for the town to remember the victims of abuse. Perhaps if this incident had not been exposed, there would have been more victims. Perhaps if I had not contributed to his demise, my demise would have been less.

Years have passed, and contact with Dr. Hoven has long been lost. The question was asked of me not long ago: "If you could say something to Dr. Hoven today, what would it be?" That answer is simple. "Forgive me! The harm I may have caused you was caused out of my own ignorance." By no means was I responsible for his actions that night. My responsibility lies in my arrogant belief that I was better than him and therefore could stand in judgment of him.

I now freely admit that I regret my actions toward the doctor. I wish I could have been one to stand with him, not in agreement with his action, but as a brother in this great universe of ours. I have learned much from my experience. We are spiritual beings living in this world. Fortunately, to gain forgiveness or get a greater understanding, all we need to do is turn in the right direction. God is love even when we choose to turn off the switch and live in darkness. When we reconnect, unconditional love flows in, and we are fulfilled.

5

When the First Domino Falls

"Greed is good!"

That line, from the movie *Wall Street*, was spoken by the character Gordon Gekko. At the end of the movie, the greedy choices he made earned him a place in prison. As my story was shared with those I cared about the most, the same fate awaited me. Greed helped me create an illusion that I was someone I wasn't. I moved away from living a life of self-integrity into living a lie.

The success I had legitimately earned was obviously not enough. My perception was that power and position came from surrounding myself with the illusions of success. Having come from "lack," my insatiable quest for "more" was no surprise. I grew up in the projects and did everything I thought I could to remove the memory of living without. It was a lesson I actively worked to create for the better part of my twenties. Whether in the body, mind, or emotions, pain was a firestorm that purified, allowing me to learn from my lessons. My most severe challenges prove to be my greatest teachers.

Over time, I have found that feelings etched early in life are hard to overcome. Striving to "be somebody" was a desire that proved to be a driving force in the conscious and subconscious decisions I made. Had I understood much earlier that I never ceased to be "somebody," perhaps life would have been dramatically different. We can't control our programming early in life; we can, however, learn that programs don't always reflect reality and, like any program, they can be changed. We are not prisoners of our past or childhood programming if we elect not to be. The choice is ours.

I never expected when the phone rang in early 1986 that I would remember the call so vividly or that it would be etched in my consciousness permanently. The choices leading up to the call were significant. The choices made following the call were life-changing. Every choice has a consequence. Little did I know, as I took the call in my office that winter day, that I would make choices that would dramatically alter and impact my life forever.

I was in the middle of planning a seminar when I was startled by the ringing of the phone. As I picked up the receiver, I heard a pleasant voice say, "Mr. Gallagher, this is Mrs. Martin at the bank. David wanted me to call and remind you your mortgage payment is due for the last two months."

Not in my wildest dreams did I expect to have that call. My relationship with the folks at the bank was outstanding, so the "Mr. Gallagher" part threw me off for a moment. Mrs. Martin was new to the bank, and we didn't know each other. However, David and I had done a fair amount of business, especially with my clients, so the formality caught me off guard. Her next comments, however, stung. "Is there a problem?" she asked.

I was a little annoyed that David didn't call me himself and relegated the task to his administrative assistant. Perhaps that was his way of avoiding conflict. The issue now was how I tell my banker, or worse, my banker's administrative assistant, that I was behind and had no prospect of catching up any time soon. I had been living beyond my means; however, admitting that to my banker when I was a prominent CPA in the community was business suicide and humiliating. I now see this call as the first opportunity to realign with my self-integrity—to right the ship. Knowing now what I didn't know then, a little humiliation at this point probably would have prevented me from taking the next step and incurring a great deal of humiliation. I heard so many times throughout my life, "Pride goes before destruction." I had a lot of pride, and I got destruction.

"Oh, Mrs. Martin, thank you for calling. I was coming by today to bring this month's payment. I've been so tied up with end of the year tax planning I just forgot. In fact, I am a little confused," I lied. "Are you sure last month's payment hasn't already been made? You know, I paid several payments in advance several months ago. Perhaps it's been misapplied." The lie just flowed from me.

The reality was I knew the payments were behind. She wasn't telling me anything I didn't already know. I just chose to fabricate my response, to lie, just to save face, and the lie came so easily. After all, how could a successful CPA allow his finances to fall into ruin while helping others successfully manage theirs? Humility failed me. My pride allowed me to maintain the illusions.

"Let me check," she responded. "Hold, please."

I don't know what I was expecting by asking her the question as I did. Perhaps a complete computer system failure would erase my erratic payment behavior, and the problem would disappear. I was just deluding myself. Because I was creating an illusion with her, it was important to let her go through the motions. I knew her response as she came back on the line saying, "No, I'm sorry. According to our records, the last two months are due."

"Thanks, Mrs. Martin. I'll be down later this afternoon or first thing in the morning to make the payment. See you then."

What now? When the conversation ended, I had to face the reality that things in my life were beginning to get out of control. I knew it, and at the moment, I was the only one who did. I wanted it to stay that way.

Placing the phone receiver in the cradle, I propped my head in my hands, wondering how I was going to make the payment I promised. My ability to borrow money was tapped. I was leveraged to the hilt. I couldn't ask my partners for an advance. They managed their money, as any good CPA should. How could I, a tax partner in the firm, admit that I couldn't manage mine? The illusion I was creating was for everybody—no one was exempt. After all, I was becoming what I thought was a "somebody," probably the greatest illusion of all.

As I sat at my desk, I thought how pleased my wife was with our new home and how things were going. I was creating for her, the community, and myself the grand illusion of success. I wanted her and our children to have the best, regardless of the cost. As often is the case, the best kept getting bigger and bigger. The new home demanded more and more new furniture, custom window treatments, landscaping. The list was endless. Everything was a money drain—money that wasn't there. I juggled bills and payments. I couldn't and wouldn't let the illusion die. My being "somebody" was too important, not only to my wife but also to me.

I stared out the window, but at what, I don't even remember. Where are the two thousand plus dollars going to come from? Telling the bank I didn't have it wouldn't work. I've already promised to make the payment. It was even more far-fetched to think about admitting to my wife that we were behind. How could I admit to her that all our surroundings were created based on leveraged debt and that we really couldn't afford them? The look on her face would have been intolerable. I rationalized that it was for her as much as anybody.

Somewhere over the course of my life, I came to believe
that being "somebody" was defined by one's surroundings, those trappings
that externally showed the world one's importance.

As I sat there, I reflected on what my mother so often told me when I was just a child: "Son, don't let your surroundings tell you otherwise; you can be somebody!" The only problem was that I seemed to have a skewed perspective of what that really meant. She never really explained what being "somebody" was about. However, somewhere over the course of my life, I came to believe that being "somebody" was defined by one's surroundings, those trappings that externally showed the world one's importance. I had the trappings, but lacked a couple of thousand dollars to make my house payment. That was a problem.

I was "somebody," and I wasn't going to let that change. I wanted to maintain that illusion, and I remember scrambling in my mind to determine how to make the payment plan. The payment was due, and I refused to let the illusion die.

As if in some stupor, I sat pondering what to do. Then it hit me. "The trust! That's it!" I thought to myself. "I'll borrow the money from my client's trust. They'll never know, and before they will ever need it, I'll pay it back." I was delighted with the solution. It would work. I had what I thought was a solution.

The choice and consequence that would eventually seal my fate were set into motion. There was a need. I needed money for my delinquent house payments, and I did not have what I perceived to be an easy resource. An opportunity presented itself. The "trust" was a vehicle available, and I had the opportunity to tap it for my needed funds. Rationalization came easily—too easily, unfortunately. I was an upstanding member of the community, and I could not be a thief. "I should borrow the money," I thought. Then with almost a level of dumb comedy, I created a dialogue with myself.

"You need to borrow some money, don't you?" I said to myself, as if I were conducting a loan interview as trustee of a private fund.

"Why, yes, actually I do. A couple of thousand will do," I replied in the beginning of this bizarre dialogue.

"Well, let me draft up a note."

As the imaginary conversation ended, I sat at the computer, booted up the word-processing program, and began to type. The illusion would not be complete without first finishing that touch that would eliminate my guilt. After all, a note is evidence of a loan, and a loan isn't theft. I wasn't a liar and a thief. I was just borrowing money, I rationalized to myself. With that thought, I concocted a scheme to get the money I needed. Undetected, I could keep the illusion alive and hedge my current needs on my future success.

Drafting the note didn't finish the illusion. Having made the choice to become a liar and thief, I completed the illusion by making the house payment and blaming my wife. In the bank later that afternoon, I approached my banker's administrative assistant with check in hand, figuring it was time to get to know her. I said, "Please convey to David my apologies. I can't believe that this slipped through. You know, we just had our first child and, well, with the challenge of a new baby and the holiday season, I suppose it just slipped her mind. She pays the bills!"

I became a little startled as David approached from behind. He had overheard most of what I said as I talked to Mrs. Martin. He saw me enter and wanted to say "Hi." As I extended my hand, in a kindhearted gesture I'll never forget, he said, "Don't worry about it. Heck, I passed a bad check once when I was in college."

We both laughed. No harm. The illusion was complete.

I was wrong in blaming my wife. Other than admitting I was less than "somebody," it was the only way. From the time we met, I was not what she wanted. I knew it; she told me. I've no idea why she married me, since I wasn't her "prince." In order to compensate, I created illusions that I was someone different. I may not have been who she wanted, but apparently I was successful in my attempts to buy her love and her affection. She stayed with me and enjoyed everything I gave her. The illusion was not solely her fault. I was the one who was insecure, and I needed to create a diversion so no one else knew my self-worth was low. Through the illusions, I found strength. I didn't have to be real as long as I was being someone else.

Regardless of the motivation, I had tipped the first domino. Set into motion was a process that the consequence would take years to realize. Slowly at first, the dominos dropped. Time would provide the momentum to fully develop an outcome that would become more painful than I could have ever imagined.

How many of us live some form of illusion in order to avoid dealing with the pain of who we are or the emotional issues that have long ago been stuffed away, hidden deeply from view? Breaking through the illusion takes courage. Willingness to be ourselves is not always easy. In many ways, we often don't know who we are, or we repudiate certain aspects of ourselves. Learning about ourselves means going to hidden places and finding the courage to enter the dark recesses of our mind and soul. When we do, then we come to understand that we are more than what we seem, and we begin the process of learning to truly love ourselves as well as others.

At that stage of my life, I didn't have the courage or the desire to go deep within myself. Frankly, I didn't even think about it. I was more comfortable living the illusion of being someone else than dealing with the consequences of being me. If I didn't like who I was without the illusions, how could anyone else? After all, my wife didn't like me without the illusions. I just didn't realize that I, like almost everyone, had areas of self-worth, and that low self-worth was my inner trapping that provided the foundation of the illusion.

I'm not alone in maintaining illusion. My uncle abused alcohol. The consequences were painful for his mother and father, his brothers and sister, and especially his wife and children. In fact, his choices cost him his family. Time after time, he had the opportunity to make different choices, and, time after time, he created the illusion of change while hiding his booze in the children's play toys or other obscure places. He worked harder on creating the illusion than he worked on changing his choices. Yet, changing his choices was the only thing that would create the outcome that could eliminate the illusion. Once again, low self-worth was the internal trapping creating the foundation for the illusions.

I recall watching his life slowly being destroyed and thinking, "How sad!" Yet, just like him, I was doing the same thing, only my destructive tool was money. As I made this one profound choice, the dominos fell, and once started, they would not stop.

At various times, we all experience windows of opportunity or intersections for choice and change. During these times, there may be many possible futures. We may be aware of these potential outcomes. Most times, however, we remain in a state of fog, not clearly seeing what our choices will yield as an outcome. How wonderful it would be if we could stop and take the time to explore fully the outcomes of these probabilities. That concept is what has been called "consequential thinking." By listening to our inner guidance and letting go of limiting thinking, we can explore many possibilities. This choice could yield this consequence. On the other hand, that choice could provide something entirely different. Unfortunately, I didn't take the time to listen to my inner voice.

"How do we learn to listen?" This is a question I have asked myself, and still do at times. The first step is to become aware of and accept who we really are in our humanity. We are created as unique beings, and as unique beings, we have unique experiences and unique journeys. We have to trust our own uniqueness and recognize that the messages we receive come in ways other than a "burning bush." Our connection to the Creator comes from within. By paying attention to our inner senses, intuition, and imagination, we receive guidance. Furthermore, there are people who cross our path simply to give us a message to aid us in our journey.

> We have to trust our own uniqueness and recognize that
> the messages we receive come in ways other than a "burning bush."

For many of us, paying attention to our inner senses or intuition is difficult. Many times this task is hampered because we don't find time to relax and be still. We are so busy with working, achieving success, and raising families that being still is an unknown concept. Coupled with that, especially in our modern Western society, we are not taught to give validity to our feelings or the inner voice. Instead, we are taught to learn by observing, using our external senses and scientific verification. For this reason, the idea of trusting intuition, something unseen, is foreign to many of us. Just because it can't be seen, however, doesn't mean it doesn't exist. We cannot see the wind or air. Yet, when we see the movement of leaves or hear the rustle in the trees, we know the air is stirring and the breeze is blowing. We trust that without question.

In the same way, when we listen and apply what we hear in a spirit-filled way, our understanding increases as the veil is lifted slightly. At that point, our relationship to everything changes. With progression comes responsibility, and part of that progression is learning to listen. When the listening is done with good intention, an amazing flood of guidance will be given.

For me, the flood of guidance provided in many different forms was always there. Like so many, I just wasn't paying attention, and therefore, I was not receptive. Instead of recognizing that right attitudes make the successful man, I elected to ignore the truth I felt in my heart. I chose to go for the outward appearance. I didn't trust my heart. I felt insecure, and my choices at the time reflected my feelings of insecurity. If I were secure enough within myself and secure enough to trust the truth, I would not have had to define myself to other people by acquiring external justification. I would have understood that being "somebody" was an inside-out job.

Several years later, I had an opportunity to share my story with a group of young people. I said, "It was never my intention to steal from and lie to people, but I did. Think about it. No one who drinks starts out intending to be a common drunk or alcoholic. Likewise, when your friends push you to try drugs—because they say it's cool—your intent is not to become a drug addict. All I wanted was to be 'somebody,' and with the money, I had all the trappings of success. But you know, kids, the more I had, the less of a 'somebody' I became. Being 'somebody' begins on the inside. I'm not proud to say this, but from that small start, from that two-thousand-dollar theft, I ended up taking over two hundred thousand dollars in less than four short years."

One choice, then another, then another, and together you weave a life. The last domino was falling, and I realized there was no stopping forward momentum. I was not in control. The control I perceived was only an illusion. I gave up control the moment I lied to the banker's assistant. I could not undo what I had done. A power greater than I would be needed to help me clean up the wretched mess I had created by moving away from self-integrity.

6

Somebody Bigger than You and I

———◆———

"Can I share this with someone?" Bob asked. My first thought was, "Why not? Everyone in the community will know it soon enough. Why not start the process?" Afternoon turned into early evening, and the emotional roller coaster was in full swing. From fear of the future, to anger about what I had done, to concern for our family, both my wife and I had run the emotional gauntlet. Within hours of my coming home, we both decided that we needed help and called our minister.

At this point, I had no clue what he could do. I had created this extraordinary drama, and frankly, I didn't see that his praying with us would change a thing. Nothing else I had done worked. I was fresh out of ideas and truly at rock bottom. I wasn't sure about the minister; however, if it made my wife feel better, what was the harm? I believed in God; what I didn't believe in was some miracle that would somehow make this problem go away. In my mind, a miracle would be rewinding the clock, which was not going to happen. The conversation with my partners, or should I say former partners, made clear that I had made very human choices, and there would be very human consequences to follow. The process had started and, like a roller coaster, once started there was no stopping the forward momentum. I had no reason to believe anything contrary to doom.

When Reverend Bob asked if he could share this with someone, there was no logical answer but "sure." Living in a small town of less than ten thousand, I knew that nothing would keep this news secret. I saw what had happened with the doctor just a year ago. I saw how bad news spread like wildfire. This would be no different. One person would tell another, then another, and soon everyone would have a spin on what happened to me and my family just as they did with the good doctor.

People seem to focus their attentions on the miseries of others. Perhaps that affords a brief opportunity to focus on someone other than themselves and those prisons that bind them. People feel better about their lives at the expense of others. Often the person who points the finger first, or is most incensed by another's misfortune, has significant issues himself. The attention focused on others' misfortunes moves the spotlight. We all have an innate desire to appear as good people, and if we can maintain an illusion to support that, we certainly will.

My wife and I both trusted Reverend Bob. He was a kind man, genuine in his beliefs, and practical in applying them. If there was anyone who would break the news to the community, even if it was communicated in confidence, Bob would be my choice. We knew that he had our best interests at heart. What Bob didn't know was the extent to which I had created a financial house of cards that was rapidly going to collapse. Little did I know that the simple question Rev. Bob asked would prove to be a key to unlock the kingdom.

A quarter of a million dollars embezzled and what to show for it? The home we lived in was, of course, mortgaged. Living the illusion meant the home we lived in was not sufficient. While we lived comfortably in one home, we had another home under construction with a loan on it. Like most middle-class American families, we had two cars, mine an upscale BMW; both, of course, were laden with debt. The assets we had were pledged for outstanding debt, debt amounting to almost five hundred thousand dollars.

I had a firm grasp of the magnitude of what was ahead. I'm not sure at that time that my wife did, which probably helped her get through this time. The future was daunting, seemingly insurmountable; frankly, it was more than I felt I could bear. The weight of the world was on my shoulders, and I was truly the only one responsible. The only short-term relief I had was that it was the weekend, and all financial institutions were closed. Perhaps if I could find some time to rest, I might have the energy to face what was ahead. Most people who knew me said that I was blessed with abundant energy, but the swirl of activity that took place over the past several days had drained me.

Having seen folks before who were in the midst of crisis, I didn't comprehend why it was so difficult for them to make the right decision From the outside looking in, it seems so easy. Not until I was in that crisis did I fully appreciate just how difficult it is to stay focused on those choices which will yield the most beneficial outcomes to me and those I touch. What is true, however, is that while in crisis, I learned I could focus. Making right choices may be difficult, but not impossible. I learned compassion for people through my experience—for that, I am grateful.

My wife asked me time after time, "What are we going to do?" That was an excellent question. Honestly, at the time, I didn't know. I didn't want to tell her that, but I really did not have a clue. Although I understood her asking, part of me wanted her not to ask because nothing changed with the questions.

I reviewed the grave situation we were in. A house under construction with a large construction loan—not many people would want to buy that. After all, it's not their design, and those who might spend that kind of money would build a custom home of their choosing. We'd have to sell our house. With no job, I certainly could not afford to keep it, but a house for sale by someone who can't afford it and is apt to lose it won't sell for much of a premium, if any. Then, there were the cars. We had to have transportation, but a BMW 745 is not a necessity. Unfortunately, the private party sales price was less than what was owed on it. Last but not least, I still owed a quarter of a million dollars to people who, at that moment, had just been informed of my transgression. They were not happy.

"What are we going to do?" my wife repeated.

"It'll all work out," I tried to say with confidence. She knew me. She just sat there staring back at me, thoroughly drained. She knew that I had lied up to this point. Why should she believe me now? Yet, I was the only hope she had. She had nowhere else to turn. She had information overload, and I was exhausted.

I felt powerless. Nothing was in my control, and I wasn't accustomed to being out of control. I truly was living the consequences of my choices, and I wasn't enjoying it. Not only was I experiencing the consequences, but so were the community and my family. I felt completely helpless with little hope to climb out of this pit.

Often we have to hit rock bottom before we can relinquish control, before we understand that we don't have the power, and that perhaps we never did. It was only another illusion. As long as I felt that I could work my way out of the mess I created, I continued to create a mess. When I became aware that I was powerless and that a power greater than I would have to fix what I had created, then I could open myself up to grace.

What does opening myself up to grace mean to me? I recalled from the Bible, "Ask, and you will receive."(John 16:24) That seems easy, but as long as I allowed my conscious self to think I was in control, I did not see the wisdom in asking for God's help. As long as I allowed my ego and my pride to take control, I stood in the way of the grace of God working in my life. Only when I realized that I had no control did I open to God's grace, and by that very act, I was back in self-integrity and thus, truly in control. My thoughts and my actions had sent my life whirling out of control, and the only option for any semblance of order was found outside of me. How I ached for the pain my family had to live through because of my choices—so many regrets. What good could come out of any of this?

I slept through the night, but it was not a restful sleep; rather, it was sleep based on exhaustion. I recall being awakened by the phone and realizing, with despair, what another day would bring. I just wanted to hide and not even face the day. What could possibly be any different today than yesterday? I now understood why some people run from their problems, knowing that to face the problems forces them to confront themselves again and again. I had looked in the mirror and did not like what I saw, and it was incredibly painful. At that moment, just as I was reaching to answer the phone, my son jumped on the bed and said, "Daddy, I love you!" I wanted to cry. The power of unconditional love is given by grace, and the next words that were spoken showed me that again.

The power of unconditional love is given by grace.

"Chuck? This is Bob." Somehow I didn't expect a call from my minister so early in the morning. Frankly, I didn't really expect a call from him. Perhaps I thought he'd made his obligatory appearance, offered prayer, and left, thinking, "What a mess he's created." How easy that would have been for him. With all the problems people faced in the community, mine was self-inflicted and certainly would not be very popular. Contrary to what I thought, Bob took a keen interest in his flock.

"Chuck, I talked to Jerry last night, and I think, if you're open to it, he'd like to talk to you. Are you interested?"

"Of course," I stammered. Normally I was articulate, but my command of words had begun to falter. Over the past several days, I had been required to reveal a new side of who I was, a shadow side and not one I was proud of. No longer did I feel I could I hold my head high. As each day passed, I was sharing who I had been with more people. I watched their faces turn to disappointment.

I tried to keep in mind that we all can make mistakes, but we are not our mistakes. For the most part, those were only words, shallow words, with the illusion of forgiveness. I felt that I was the mistake, and everyone I talked with seemed to agree. I was confident that anyone who has ever had to face admitting shortcomings, mistakes, screwups, or whatever we characterize the poor choices from our past, knows the shameful feeling that accompanies our admission. I was feeling deeply shameful, and my self-worth was way on the negative side.

Perhaps we avoid admitting our mistakes because the process is painful. Stripping back the layers of our ego, that part of us that we've taken years to create, isn't comfortable. It takes a willingness to know ourselves, and it takes courage to admit the shadow side of ourselves. Sometimes, knowing our dark side comes from the stark reality of being thrown off the roller coaster of life. More times than not, we don't choose to look at ourselves when the opportunities arise. Many years and many choices create the illusion, and we don't find the core of our being all at once. When we break through our illusions and return to self-integrity, we realize that we need help. Only then can we be open to the process of healing. As I heard Rev. Bob's voice, I was open to whatever he had to offer. The one thing I knew for sure was that I needed to let go. My life was messed up by my own actions, and it was time to "let go and let God."

I wasn't sure what would happen at the meeting Bob proposed. The only thing I knew was that I had nothing to lose. The meeting was set for Sunday evening.

As I arrived at Jerry's house, I was steps away from the unknown. I was not a stranger since Jerry and his wife went to my church, and Jerry and I were in Rotary together. We both spoke the Rotary pledge even as I knew I practiced the opposite of what it stood for. While I was proud of my membership and what the organization stood for, it was part of the illusion. Jerry was well respected, and I was privileged to have a meeting with him. My only question was why he would want to meet with me, especially after what Bob must have told him. The only way to know for sure was to take the first step. I stepped out of my car, asked God for guidance, and rang the bell.

I was welcomed in by Jean, who was a lovely and kind hostess. She never revealed any disgust. Instead, she kindly asked me if I wanted anything to drink. She drifted away, leaving Jerry and me to talk alone. No doubt she knew the story and was kind enough not to mention it.

"Bob shared that you have some trouble. Is there anything you want to share with me?" Jerry asked in a quiet, kind voice. His voice elicited trust from me.

Frankly, I didn't know what to say. I didn't know what Jerry was looking for, but I felt fairly certain he already knew some of the truth. For that matter, I wasn't even sure why I was there. Over the past few days, people, events, and things in general were whirling by too fast and felt out of control. The feeling of being out of control was unfamiliar and uncomfortable. As a result, my ability to be my normal articulate, calculating self seemed to have vanished, leaving me in uncharted territory. I took a deep breath and looked into Jerry's eyes.

"Jerry, I've screwed up." And with those words, I shared my story of deceit. I lost track of time as I opened up myself and my emotions to this man who listened seemingly without judgment. Tears flowed down my face, and I was too exhausted even to care anymore. The emotional release that came from opening the truth to Jerry was amazing.

I don't know what he expected from me. Perhaps it was a test of sorts. Could I move past my ego and accept my humanity? Would I allow myself to be vulnerable and show the world the truth of who I was versus the illusion I had masterfully created? To this day, I have never asked Jerry what he expected from me that night, but it was a turning point in my life.

As the conversation was winding down, the only thing I recall Jerry saying was, "Do you mind if we pray?" With that question, seemingly out of nowhere, Jean reappeared. We all sat, holding hands as Jerry spoke to God.

I do not recall the prayer. All I recall is the feeling. There was a power that seemed to emanate from Jerry and his wife that felt much like unconditional love. It was the first time during the past several days that I had experienced any compassion. As the meeting ended, Jerry and Jean escorted me to the door, and I felt better as I walked to my car.

> I exposed myself, revealing who I was and laying the groundwork for who I could become. Shedding the skin of my past illusions was somehow refreshing.

I sat for a moment, noticing I had been in their home for hours. The hour was late, and I knew that my wife would be wondering what had happened. Frankly, I wondered what happened. There was no magic solution offered, just a willing ear and a heartfelt prayer. For once—once in a long time—I felt good. I exposed myself, revealing who I was and laying the groundwork for who I could become. Shedding the skin of my past illusions was somehow refreshing. I didn't think, though, that was what my wife would want to hear.

"What did he say?" was her first question as I entered the door. I don't know what she expected. Perhaps we both were looking for a "quick-fix savior"—someone or something that would take this burden away from us. That was not to be.

"Well, I told him what I had done, and then we prayed," I replied.

"That's it? That's all?" Sitting for hours alone, wondering what was taking place, had taken its toll on her. As if she wasn't frazzled enough by my revelations, which were just now really starting to sink in. "Is he going to help us?"

She had asked a question I could not answer. I could only shrug my shoulders. After all, what could he do? I had no hope. I had created this mess, and I, and those with whom I was connected closely, would suffer the consequences. The Bible says, "You will reap what you sow." I had sowed powerful illusions, so I suspected that the reaping of consequences would be just as powerful. I believed in the power of God, but I also believed that one would suffer for one's transgressions, and boy, had I transgressed. I didn't feel worthy of anything else.

Within a day or two I was surprised by a call from Jerry.

"Chuck, this is Jerry. Can we talk? How about us getting together later today?"

"Sure," I replied. "Just tell me when and where."

I downplayed the meeting as I told my wife where I was going. At this stage, the one thing I knew was that I had completely destroyed any trust that my wife had in me. Now wasn't the time to create false beliefs or false illusions. It was the only protection I could offer her at that moment. Furthermore, I had no idea what Jerry wanted. It was best to not create any hope in her.

Upon arrival and after exchanging short pleasantries, Jerry asked with a deep sincerity how both my wife and I were doing. Jean spoke up, acknowledging that it had to be hard on us all. I could feel the depth of her concern and compassion. "Chuck, Jean and I were thinking about building a new home, something on one level. We drove over to the house that you and your wife have under construction. We love it. It's perfect for us. In fact, we were looking at house plans and found something almost identical. Would you and your wife consider allowing us to buy it from you, to take over the debt you have in the house and let us finish it for ourselves?"

I couldn't believe my ears! I was dumbfounded. How could this be? What I just heard coming from Jerry's mouth was a miracle. He and his wife wanted to take an albatross off our hands. I still couldn't believe my ears. Who in their right minds would want to buy a house in mid-construction and finish it for their own?

"Jerry, what I just heard you offer is a gift from God!" I stated, hoping that he would not withdraw his offer. Instead, he had another question.

"What are you and your wife going to do with the home you live in now?"

"I don't know. We can't afford to keep it. I suppose we'll move in with my mother-in-law. Why do you ask?"

I had no idea what he'd say, but thus far, in less than fifteen minutes Jerry's offer had eliminated over a quarter of a million dollars in debt that was weighing heavily on my mind.

His next comments floored me. What was unfolding before me was the power of God at work. It wasn't an immediate and complete lesson, but one that started a process to show just what was possible when one gets out of the way and allows the power of the universe to flow. Jerry shared that his son Ken was on the market for both a new house and a new car. Ken was willing to pay appraised value for both our existing home and my automobile. To say the least, I was shocked. In less than an hour, for fair value, this family had removed nearly a half million dollars of debt from my back, and done so in a fair and honest manner.

You reap what you sow! How true. Perhaps in some divine way, I was being given a message. I could not undo the consequences that would follow the extraordinary choices I made. That reaping was yet to come and had only begun to unfold at this point. Yet, I was to find out later that my honesty with Jerry that first evening was the catalyst that opened the door for the blessings that were heaped upon my family. Had I made a different choice that night, an ego-centered choice, I am confident that the outcome would have been dramatically different.

Over the course of the next three months, miracle after miracle unfolded. Not only was the burden of debt on my houses and automobiles removed, but Jerry offered me a job. Humbled by the outpouring of kindness, I was overwhelmed that someone would look beyond my faults and once again place trust in me. Mind you, my income was reduced by well over $100,000 a year, but I was glad to have a job.

Within a week after revealing my misdeeds to my partners, I relinquished my license as a CPA to the State Board of CPA Examiners. There was no purpose in fighting what would be an inevitable outcome. I would lose my license. In my mind, I was just as well off to give it up voluntarily. Perhaps accepting responsibility would account for something as the consequences began to unfold systematically. As a Continuing Professional Education instructor, I sought the consent of the State CPA Board to allow me to continue to teach as a means to make restitution.

As I stepped back into self-integrity, doors opened, and hope began to blossom. Friends and family rallied around me, creating an opportunity to gather the money needed to make restitution. The State Board suspended the revocation of my license, allowing me the limited opportunity to teach Continuing Professional Education courses, a means to earn funds necessary to make restitution. Most importantly, the local District Attorney didn't find it necessary to prosecute. After all, I had lost my license, lost my job, and lost my reputation. There seemed to be no benefit to yet another loss—my freedom.

Christmas wasn't the same in 1990. I had no funds to buy presents that heretofore had been lavished on my wife and children. I remember doing the only thing for her that I could, making a homemade video—a collage of pictures of our family placed to music. This was my way of saying that love isn't about the things, but about the people who are special in our life. It touched my heart to make it. I fear that mine was the only heart it touched. It was evident that I had destroyed the faith and hope in my wife.

Each day was fraught with one challenge or another. There was no magic wand that made things better, that took away the pain, shame, guilt and hurt that was felt daily. My wife's distrust was evident with every glance. I was looked at differently from the community. However, I survived it all and have a better life because of it. The lessons are never far from my mind. I remember that true humility, true control, lies in knowing that there is a power greater than I.

7

Just How Taxing Can This Be?

The past seven months had been tough. Each day seemed like an eternity, especially at the beginning, when I first exposed my true colors. The consequences mounted quickly at first and seemed insurmountable and felt as if they were more than I could bear. Each day brought its own challenges, and rarely was there a moment when some thought of my misdeeds and the consequences I was living through were not on my mind.

I heard an unexpected steady knock at the front door but thought it must be someone peddling something door-to-door. So I sat in my chair, continuing to watch TV with no intention of answering. After all, they had nothing that I wanted. I didn't need religious pamphlets as I was comforted in my faith and by my church and, considering all that had transpired over the past seven or so months, I certainly couldn't afford to buy anything.

As I sat quietly waiting for my unexpected visitors to move on to the next house, I thought about my return to work and to some sense of normalcy. I expected to lose my job. I expected to lose my license as a CPA. Beyond that I didn't know what to expect. As usually happens, time had passed and many of the unknowns, issues, and trials that I brought onto myself had been resolved. While I was constantly aware that I was an embezzler and that I committed the crimes, after seven or so months, most of the major issues seemed to have been resolved.

Sure enough, as I had expected back then, I had been fired. That was no great surprise. I lost my license. I had made many of my clients angry due to my theft of their assets. Most importantly, and probably the greatest consequence, was that I had destroyed the trust my wife and family had in me. I sighed deeply, realizing that there was no one in my life, business or personal, who was left untouched by my choices. Even though I had endured the loss of so much, exposing myself in a true and honest manner proved to be a turning point in the process of recovery, and that was the most profound positive result of the entire experience. It was the starting point of paying it forward.

Looking back, I can clearly see that as soon as I spoke the truth, as painful as it was, the flow of redemptive help began to flow. While I lost my license as a CPA, the State Board of CPA Examiners, realizing that restitution was critical, worked with me to allow me to use my skills teaching and speaking so that I could generate income legally and ethically to make the restitution I desired. There were consequences, but there were also open doors to begin anew.

While I didn't come from a wealthy family, I found that honesty allowed me to shed the illusion I created so that family and friends could rally around the "real me." I was "somebody," I just didn't know it when shrouded in illusion. When I shed the illusion, it became much easier to receive help. Because of the decision to live and to live in integrity, the collective power of the grace and love that flowed provided the resources to make restitution to those I defrauded.

Though I felt undeserving of help, loved ones made sacrifices, sacrifices that were financially painful. Each wanted to help. My grand-mother-in-law, my mother-in-law, my mother, and several friends stepped forward either to loan me money or help me legitimately borrow money to make restitution. I didn't have to walk this road alone. My family, in spite of their hurt and disappointment, was willing to walk with me.

A dear friend and mentor, Lynn, said to me in a resonant and calm voice, "I am here for you. I am here to help you. People were there for me when I needed them, so I am here for you."

He was not the only one who stepped forward. The collective power of love was shown by these people, who had every right to turn their backs and let me face my consequences alone. However, they saw beyond the crime to the real man inside and expressed love and forgiveness in many different ways. This man inside of me, from whom I fled because of feelings of unworthiness, was the man that people responded to out of love. My crime taught me the lesson of my own value, my own worthiness. Often, through the valleys of our lives, we learn the greatest lessons.

> My crime taught me the lesson of my own value,
> my own worthiness. Often, through the valleys of our lives,
> we learn the greatest lessons.

By May of 1991, the financial and legal process was drawing to a positive conclusion. I will never forget the anxiety and pending sense of potential relief as I walked into the attorney's office to sign the paperwork to make full and complete restitution, with interest, to those I defrauded. I longed to make peace with this chapter of my life and put together new beginnings for me and my family.

These people didn't like me—that was obvious from the comments that came from them through their attorneys. I had let them down and betrayed their trust. They were disappointed and hurt. The energy of money was strong in people's lives. My advantage was that they wanted their money more than they wanted me prosecuted. I couldn't repay if I couldn't work. Aside from that, on a very human note, some of those I defrauded showed compassion toward me and my family. One said, "He suffered enough. I don't want his children to have to visit him in jail." That compassion was undeserved, yet appreciated, and I accepted it.

I would at times slip off to sleep late at night in simple amazement at the compassion and love that people seemed to be willing to share. *What have I done to deserve such kindness?* I thought. I felt unworthy of their kindness.

The paperwork was signed. The money was collected and deposited into my attorney's trust account. As I walked out the door on that May spring day, I knew a phase of my life was passing and that the time to rebuild had begun. I paused as I stepped out the door, taking in a deep breath and slowly releasing it, as I believed the worst was behind me. Perhaps now I could walk into my future.

With one exception, I never spoke to the clients or their representatives again. Not that I was unwilling to speak to them; rather, I was ashamed to speak with them. They didn't initiate contact with me nor, because of my feelings of shame, did I with them. I was guilty and felt the pain and weight of that guilt. I saw no value or reason for continued communication. After all, I was a clear reminder that blind trust can be deceiving. I don't think they willingly received that lesson. Rather, with restitution made, they could close a chapter in their lives, a chapter I'm sure they were glad to get behind them.

I had done tax return work for the local district attorney, and while his job was to prosecute criminals, he elected not to prosecute me. Perhaps he believed that the consequences had been severe enough. Perhaps he saw I had made restitution and lost everything else. Perhaps he had compassion for my family and felt nothing was to be gained from incarcerating me. Or, perhaps I had done a good job in the tax work I had done for him, and this was his way of paying it back. Whatever the reason, I was relieved to know that criminal prosecution was going to be avoided.

"You're lucky," my attorney stated to me. "I've seen very few people avoid prosecution, especially when the district attorney has such an open and shut case. You should feel very lucky."

Feel, I thought to myself. *I don't know what or how to feel.* For so long, each day had come with its own stress. Not a day went by from January through May of 1991 that I didn't feel the pain of guilt and the stress and weight of the unknown. *Lucky?* I thought to myself. I felt anything but lucky. I felt I got the consequences I earned, but it could have been much worse. Lucky? Yes, I was lucky. I wasn't going to prison.

By now, it was midsummer, and I was beginning to focus more on work and putting the pieces of my life back together. I had moved, so I thought, through the worst of my experience and began focusing some on the future. My marriage was in shambles. I was doing all I could do to rebuild trust, something that truly seemed elusive and would later become completely impossible. I wanted my marriage. I wanted my wife to believe in me. I wanted to lessen the effects of hurt on her. I just didn't know if I could.

On the other hand, my complete change in lifestyle had one unexpected benefit: I was home each night with my children. My oldest was four years old, going on five, and full of boundless energy. At that age, he could play for hours, and with summer evenings dragging darkness closer to nine, I found out just how easy it was to be worn out from being my son's horse.

Finding joy in the middle of crisis and chaos is difficult. Every time I would look into my wife's eyes, I saw doubt and disappointment. She wanted to be supportive, but couldn't get out of her mind the deceit and the feelings of betrayal. Only ten years earlier, she had been faced with deceit from another man close to her, and now I had sealed her belief that men couldn't be trusted. I regret to this day the scar my actions left. The only thing I could think of was that by my making different choices now, perhaps she would believe. I could only hope the damage was short-term for her.

"Daddy, let's play horse again." Down on my knees I would go as Rob would run and jump on my back. We'd take off, and he would squeal with delight.

My son knew that things were different. We didn't live in the same house that was familiar to him, the house he came home to from birth. He knew that Mommy was upset but wasn't sure why. He knew that Daddy didn't travel anymore. We didn't want him to feel it was his fault, as kids often feel when there is trouble in the home. We wanted him to feel safe and secure in the knowledge he was loved and cared about by his parents. We were both committed to being good parents to our children. With them, especially with them, we focused on their needs. The biting comments and anger were reserved, as much as possible, for our time alone together.

My other son, Alex, was just past a year old and truly wasn't affected in the same way Rob was. He had no memory of his former home, no memory of Dad traveling. The environment he found himself in seemed normal. And, for all practical purposes, it was.

My choices had devastating personal consequences, but one thing I had committed to was making sure that my sons weren't scarred deeply. My illusion was that this was having no effect on them, but I knew too well that illusions can be painful when stripped back to reality. Yet, I believed that positive, loving choices can heal old scars. While we may not be able to change our choices from the past, we can make choices now and in the future that can heal. I remain, today, committed to healing those scars.

The bond that exists between my children and me is strong, loving, and committed. I have hidden nothing from them about who I am today, the events of my past, and the intense love I feel for them. Sure, we've had our moments, as most fathers and sons have. However, I have worked hard to make choices that will serve them and teach them a foundation of honesty, respect, and love for themselves and others so that they won't be permanently scarred from any of my past choices.

While I was in contemplation about some of my poor choices, the visitors at my front door persisted in their effort to get my attention.

Then the doorbell rang, as if to let me know they were going nowhere. I just wanted to be left alone.

As I moved toward the door, silently I slipped up and looked through the peep hole to see who was outside. I had already concluded that unless it was a Boy Scout, I wasn't going to answer.

Reluctantly, I slowly opened the door. "Yes. Can I help you?"

"Are you Charles Gallagher?" one of the men asked sternly.

Now, the way I see it, nothing good comes from someone asking you who you are by your first-given "Christian" name. Rather, that's the kind of thing you would hear from your mama when you were in trouble. You know exactly what I mean. You went outside and played in the mud when your mother told you not to. Then you came in and, despite your best efforts, you tracked mud in the house. Then you hear that call that only a mother can make. "Charles B. Gallagher, get yourself down here right now!"

"Yes. I'm Chuck Gallagher," I replied to the men at my front door. I would have preferred to say I was anyone but Chuck Gallagher. The man's voice sounded ominous. I had a gut feeling that being Chuck Gallagher right now meant there was trouble afoot.

Almost simultaneously, they reached into their jacket pockets and pulled out two shiny gold badges, sticking them into my face as their identification. One identified himself as from the Criminal Investigation Division of the Department of Labor and the other, the Criminal Investigation Division of the Internal Revenue Service.

Being face-to-face with two gold badges and the seriousness of the men behind them had me dazed.

The only thing I recall from that immediate moment was how well-crafted and shiny their gold badges were. The sun glistened and danced off their polished beveled edges. I know that it seems utterly foolish to recall only the badges, but I had come to believe that the consequences, at least those of significance, were behind me. Restitution had been made, and no one cared about my prosecution, so being face-to-face with two gold badges and the seriousness of the men behind them had me dazed.

"Mr. Gallagher—we're here to inform you that you are the subject of a federal criminal investigation. Do you have an attorney?"

"Yes." I replied with what I know must have been a look of total surprise and confusion. Two branches of the federal government investigating me? What was there to investigate? As far as I was concerned, I had come clean, fessed up to my wrongdoings and made amends. What more could anyone want from me, especially the federal government? I would soon find out. They didn't waste any time.

The man from the Department of Labor spoke first. "You're being investigated for criminal violations of ERISA, the Employee Retirement Income Security Act of 1974. Are you familiar with what that is?" the DOL agent asked with a bit of a smirk.

I replied before I thought. It's natural to tell the truth when faced with a question that you don't expect. And I didn't expect his question. Frankly, I didn't expect him or his "friend" at my door, then or ever.

Then I remembered, possibly from cop shows. What you say can and will be used against you in a court of law. But then again, what could I say that they didn't already know? Everyone in town knew about my crime, so incriminating myself wouldn't be much of a problem. Apparently these two gentlemen knew, too, or they wouldn't be standing on my front porch.

As if the first man's comments weren't shocking and powerful enough, the second man's words ring clear to this day. "The Internal Revenue Service is conducting a criminal investigation of you for criminal tax evasion."

"Tax evasion?" I replied.

"You must know that income from all sources is taxable, even stolen money!"

I stood in stunned silence. Very few times have people who knew me claimed that I would ever be speechless. This was, however, one of those times. I never heard of such a thing. How could it be tax evasion if I am paying restitution to the families? The money is gone, and I am giving it back.

"May we have your attorney's name and contact information?"

As I stepped away from the door after giving them what they asked for, I felt what life I had seemed to regain over the past few months drain quickly away. Everything I had worked for seemed to make little difference. I felt totally hopeless. Transported back to when this whole issue came to light, I felt my throat constrict and my stomach turn to knots. What I thought was past was now looking as if it had just begun again, although this time with far more severe potential consequences. *How can I live through this? How can my family live through this?* I wondered.

Not that the past wasn't difficult. It was. It was the toughest time of my life, a life I had considered ending. Now, before the night would end, once again I would have to face my wife and family and break the news. How much more could they take?

How do you tell bad news to someone you love, someone who is hanging on by just a thread, looking for something to cling to that would bring some normalcy back to her life and the lives of her children? How do you tell that person that you might be going to jail after all? How would she survive this? As I stared out the window, wondering how to move through this, the tears that were threatening to come just came. They were tears of frustration and shame and fear of the unknown. Would my marriage survive? What about my children?

How am I going to tell my wife that the roller coaster ride is beginning again? I wondered. I knew the burden would push her beyond her capacity to survive. I had no idea what to say or how to say it. The only thing that kept coming to my mind to say was, "Guess what? Two criminal investigators came to see me today, and they want to put me in prison."

That wouldn't work. *Too harsh,* I thought. But honestly, thinking wasn't clear now. The only thing I could do was wipe tears from my eyes as I fell into a chair feeling totally exhausted and useless. Briefly, I thought about taking my own life. "Why not?" As I sat there thinking about ending my life, I heard over and over again in my mind the voice of the man on the phone that fateful night in Boise, Idaho, saying, "You've made a mistake, but you are not that mistake! What legacy will you leave for your children?" Once again, this man saved my life. If I took my life, it would be a selfish act. My children would not learn how to manage the mistakes they would inevitably make and know that they still had value apart from the mistake.

So, I took a deep breath, pulling it together. One step at a time—this was another step, and with God's help, somehow we'd make it through.

8

Miracle on South Wilmington Street

———◆———

Five months had passed since the feds had shown up on my front doorstep, unannounced and unwelcomed. In just a few weeks, it would be Christmas. I had awakened that morning much like every other morning since the feds came, wondering if today would be the day that I would find out my fate. Because I stayed in bed a few minutes longer that day, I was in a hurry to leave my home and begin the long trek to Raleigh for work. I no sooner finished closing the door to my home when the early morning silence was broken by the ringing of my cell phone.

"Chuck. This is Frank. I've got some bad news."

Damn, I thought to myself, and I asked Frank to hold just a second as I got into my car. *What is it now?* I wondered. I felt a wave of anger rise up within me. It was anger at no one in particular—probably just fear showing itself as anger. For several months, the issue of the federal investigation had been percolating, and there had been general silence. Although some say silence is golden, to me it just created a weary anticipation.

Frank was my attorney and a stabilizing factor in my life. He wasn't flamboyant like the late Johnny Cochran of O. J. Simpson fame, but rather, he was an attorney who understood the law and the legal system. He held the respect of all in the legal community, including the prosecutors.

71

Up until July 1991, I thought that all the legal issues had been resolved. There was no hint of anything contrary to resolution. Since confessing, I believed I had done everything correctly. The gold badges glistening in the sun of that summer afternoon changed all that. Now Frank was dealing with a facet of this saga that neither of us expected.

I was hungry for news, good news. Surely, I thought, they would see the wisdom of probation. After all, I had admitted my crime, made restitution, and suffered what I felt was enough. The emotional toll was mounting with the silence. So, yes, I wanted to hear something. The one thing I didn't want to hear was Frank speaking those words.

As I pulled away from my mother-in-law's home, the place I was living at the time, I reconnected with Frank. I was headed to Raleigh on a work-related trip, so I had the time and privacy to talk. Driving gave me quiet time to think and get away from the constant reminders of my failure to my family.

Although I'm confident that it wasn't intentional or mean-spirited, the truth was, my wife and mother-in-law both exuded a distrustful and judgmental attitude that bore heavily on my soul. It had a negative effect on me as I was desperately trying to regain a sense of self. I was normally an optimistic human being, and I found it incredibly difficult to regain who I was with the constant reminder that I had failed so horribly. Redemption, especially from those I sought it from the most, seemed to elude me. So, this drive to Raleigh provided time for me to heal my spirit without the constant reminder of being a failure.

"Chuck. Do you have time to take this call?" asked Frank as he heard the motor start and the car bell dinging in the background.

"Frank, I've got all the time we need. However, let's start this conversation over. I don't want any bad news."

Frank went on without acknowledging my attempt at humor. "I just received a call from the U.S. attorney handling your case. He wants you to plead guilty, and you will go to prison. All this should happen, if you agree, within the next two weeks. And Chuck, I don't know when your sentence will begin, but you might not be home for Christmas. You need to know that." Frank never minced words; he was straightforward and to the point. What he called "bad news," I called the end of the world.

I felt light-headed as Frank's words reverberated within my mind. All I could think of was, with all that had happened, how would I break this to my family? How much more could they take? The rush of emotion was choked back for the moment, and I had to finish this call. So I pushed my feelings inside and drove in stunned silence.

"Chuck, are you still there?"

"I'm here for now," I replied, feeling drained, almost dead within.

"I know this isn't what you wanted, but he's willing to allow you to plead guilty to one count of embezzlement and one count of tax evasion. It might not seem like a win, but it's much better than it could be. If he wanted to play hardball, you'd be facing over twenty years in prison. As it stands, with his offer you'd be facing eighteen months to five years." Frank was firm, but optimistic as he spoke.

Looking back at the moment, I really didn't like what I was hearing. I didn't like Frank. I didn't like the day. I didn't want to face this, not now—not ever.

> I really didn't like what I was hearing.
> I didn't like Frank. I didn't like the day. I didn't want
> to face this, not now—not ever.

As I regained some form of composure, I tried to engage in some conversation with Frank. Perhaps he had missed something in his communication with the prosecutor.

"Frank, I'm lost. I'm paying a big bank loan right now, a bank loan that people guaranteed so that I could make restitution. If I go to prison now, I can't pay that off. That's not fair to those who helped me. Surely

73

you let him know that imprisoning me now would only cause more pain to those who don't deserve it. Did you talk to him about deferred prosecution? Did you?"

I'm sure Frank could tell that my anxiety level was rising by the tone and emotion in my voice. I didn't mind pleading guilty. I accepted that it was a part of the consequence. Over time, it had become clear that any attempt to avoid accountability for one's actions would only increase the intensity of the consequences. The only way to regain a sense of my true self was to move through the process and accept the outcomes. I just thought the harsh outcomes were finished and wasn't sure how to explain to my wife.

Good God! I didn't want to face or experience prison. More importantly than that, I didn't want to create further casualties due to an overzealous prosecutor who saw me as an easy notch in his prosecutorial victories. Surely there was some compassion and reason. At least he could allow me to repay the bank before putting me behind bars.

"Frank, maybe I need to talk with him."

Honestly, that would have been a dumb move, and I think my attorney knew and guided me. But, I was grasping at straws. Somehow the outcome needed to be different. This was the wrong outcome! There had to be a way that I could change the outcome. I just had to look harder.

"Chuck, I've talked with him several times. He wanted more. He wanted to prosecute you on multiple charges and hence get a longer prison sentence. But, because you made restitution and lost your license, and due to your family situation, this is the best we could get.

"Now," Frank continued, "I need you to think about his offer and get back with me by the end of the day. I have to let him know your answer tomorrow. And Chuck, I have to advise you: this is a good offer."

With those words, the call ended. I couldn't hold back the emotion at that point. Tears streamed down my cheeks, and I had to pull over, stop driving, and just take some time to regroup. The depth of despair

I felt at that point was almost as intense as that night back in Boise, Idaho, when I first knew that my choices would have a profound consequence.

Perhaps ending my life would be best, I thought to myself in a fleeting moment. *Perhaps an auto accident.* People say when they are about to die, their life passes through their eyes in a matter of moments. I felt like I was dying as life quickly passed through my eyes, and I wished for a time that I was dead. I sat there as the thoughts seemed to fly by in random fashion, no order, no reason, just thoughts about the call and what the future held. I couldn't imagine leaving my children at such a young age and serving a prison sentence. Perhaps everyone would be better off if I just died in an auto "accident." At least they would have my life insurance. At least they would not have to endure more humiliation.

If I had ever imagined in my wildest dreams that the consequences of my actions would have been this, I would have made different choices. Then again, most people, when facing the consequences of their actions, would say the same thing. How powerful it would be if we could see the potential consequence before the choice and have the wisdom to choose those things that would further our life's purpose. I suppose, though, if we had foreknowledge, we would lose essential parts of the lesson. There would be no lesson because we would likely make the right choice.

So many times I recall my mother saying to me, "Son, you can be somebody." And, for so many years I tried "the somebody route." The problem was that I never truly knew what being "somebody" meant. I tried to become what I already was and just didn't know it. I tried though, to the best of my ability, to be that somebody. Some of my choices were good and worthwhile—they served me, and I, through them, helped others. However, the limited self-defeating choices I made far overshadowed the positive choices and the good that came from them. For now, I was in a cycle of suffering through the consequences, and just when it seemed to have an end—it didn't.

For so many years I tried "the somebody route."
The problem was that I never truly knew what
being "somebody" meant.

The trip seemed to pass quickly. I arrived at my destination without even realizing that I was driving or even making the journey. As I pulled into the parking lot of the office, I focused on regaining my composure and prepared to put on a mask to maintain the illusion at work that all was well with me.

The folks I worked with didn't know about my choices, my past, or my background. The people who hired me knew, and that was all that mattered at the time. I chose not to reveal my life to the others. In thinking about it now, I am aware that most of our time is spent in illusion—spent appearing different from what is truly real. It seems odd to me. Yet, that was the way life was for me then.

I took a deep breath and regained my composure as I walked into the office. No one knew that the news I received that morning was, perhaps to me, some of the worst I ever received. They smiled and greeted me, and I responded in like manner. I was a master illusionist.

I couldn't help thinking that day, though: how many times do we have surface connections with others, never realizing what they may be going through? There is an incredible amount of energy that goes into maintaining those illusions, and with that comes a built-in distrust of other people. We are all players in this grand game called life. From time to time, we can make a difference, if only we're willing to engage. When we're willing to look past the illusion within ourselves and other people, we just might find out that we are more, much more, than we seem. Yet so many of us choose to hide behind the illusions rather than to risk possible rejection if we reveal our true selves and our true journey.

With my mask shakily in place, I endured one of the longest days of my life. As for productivity, well, I can't say it was one of my better days. What work I did accomplish was, as much as possible, done in solitude. I just didn't seem to have the energy to interact with those around me. It was more than I had in me that day. My thoughts were consumed with what was ahead and how I would break the news to my family. I was at a loss for what to do now—for them, or for me. Once again, travel away from home, a night in a hotel room, and my trip back home would yield bad news. As fragile as my life with my wife was now, I could only imagine that this news would destroy her and any remnants of being able to rebuild our life together.

As the end of the day approached, I prepared mentally to call Frank. My inclination was not to call and continue hiding within myself. Perhaps if I didn't call, then it would only be a nightmare that would just pass me by. The truth, however, was that it was reality, and I created this reality. I knew, as I had known all day, that there was no alternative but to accept the offer. Why I waited to the last minute, I did not know.

I stared at the phone, wondering what would happen to my family. Would they survive? Would I survive? There were so many unknowns. I imagined the tears and the anger my wife would express. I imagined what it would be like to leave my boys behind. How would I ever explain that Daddy was going to jail? Deep within my soul, there was a part of me that longed for someone to see past the illusion. I felt alone. So many times since then, I have thought about how I felt and how others in similar situations feel when they move through such life changing processes.

"Chuck." The silence of my private thoughts in my makeshift office was broken by Betty's voice as she paged me on the phone intercom.

"You have a call from a Frank Gold-something on line four. I couldn't quite get his name."

"Chuck, are you near a fax machine?" were the first words out of Frank's mouth.

"Yes."

"Is it private or can you go stand by it?"

"Yes, Frank, I can do that."

"I'm getting ready to fax you a document that you need to read immediately. It's a deferred prosecution agreement. The U.S. attorney is offering to defer your prosecution for three years."

"What? I thought you told me that based on your conversation with the U.S. attorney this morning that no such offer was possible. What happened?"

"I don't know. My last conversation with him was this morning before I talked with you. I was waiting for your call so I could call him back, when just a few minutes ago, maybe thirty or so, I got a call from his office saying that they were sending over this agreement for me to review.

"Chuck, this is what I received. Now, are you near a fax machine? Because I have to respond today."

How could a decision change that dramatically in the scope of six or so short hours? Only this morning I was to be prosecuted and punished quickly; now this afternoon, I have an offer deferring my punishment for three years. It was nothing short of a miracle.

"Chuck, this agreement is fourteen pages. I've never seen an agreement like this done in such a short time. Now, go by your machine and call me back if you don't get it all. I'll be waiting."

I left the comfort of my solitude and stood by the fax machine with an almost gleeful anticipation. I doubt most people would be gleeful about agreeing to prosecution and possible imprisonment, but in my case, I was. This miraculous change was nothing short of incredible. I had said many times that I was prepared to accept the consequences of my actions, but, likewise, I felt that those conse-quences should not adversely affect those who stood beside me in a time of need. This change, this miracle, made it possible for me to accept financial responsibility for my actions and give the government a win as well.

And, as hope can grow from a small seed, who knew, but perhaps the government will see the fruit of my actions and elect not to prosecute or not to incarcerate. At that moment, I didn't know. What I did know was, as the fourteen pages were spitting out one after the other, something cosmically changed. My attorney did nothing different. I did nothing different, but the end of the day brought about a different reality than the one that the day started with.

Sometimes the consequences from our actions can be quite profound. Some of us don't want to accept that we have any responsibility for what is happening to us or happening around us. However, over the years, through many examples, I came to see that every choice has a consequence—some microscopic, and some so powerful that they are life changing. We can't time the consequences or, in many ways, determine how they might take place. Some might beat us up and emotionally weigh us down. Others come in unexpected packages.

As the final pages came though the fax machine, I came to believe that this miracle on Wilmington Street, the area in Raleigh where I worked, was happening as a result of my powerful choices made to be real, to be honest, to accept responsibility, and to understand that God knows I am "somebody!"

A miracle accepted. I signed the agreement and a new chapter began.

9

Every Choice Has a Consequence

<hr>

"Dad, get up. Let's go open presents."

My younger son was generally the first up on Christmas morning, full of joy and anticipation. His life-spirit was always something that I deeply admired. No matter what was happening, he found something positive to talk about or focus on, turning attention away from the negative.

For almost all of his life, our family had been embroiled in the consequences of my past actions. That certainly weighed heavily on my wife; by this time, our marriage was disintegrating, as I expected it would after the news that I would go to prison at some point. Likewise, my older son was much more aware that things had changed in our family. While my wife and I worked hard to make sure they knew it had nothing to do with them, I am sure that it took as much an emotional toll on them as it did on us.

"Come on, Dad, get up!"

By Christmas 1994, three years had passed since I received that fax deferring my prosecution. I knew I'd been given a gift when my attorney had called, sharing that joyous news several years earlier. What I didn't know was just how significant the choices made during that span of time would be.

Intellectually, I understood the concept of choices and consequences, but on a deeper emotional level I still didn't grasp the bigger picture—perhaps because I didn't want to face the bigger picture. The threat of prosecution looming over me was an emotionally draining experience. Not a day would go by that I wouldn't think about it and feel that pain in the pit of my stomach. I didn't know how I could face it. There were times when I wanted to give up. What difference would it make, anyway? I would sometimes lapse into a pit of self-pity. I had lost my reputation, my job, my home, my income, and likely, my family. *For what?* I wondered. The outcome was still the same: PRISON. There were times when I wondered if it might not have been better to have just taken the punishment and spiraled into a life with no future, accepting the role of convicted felon.

Then there were times, in fact most of the time, that I was so thankful for the additional time that I had received. It provided me the time to begin to repay the loans to the people who had helped me. It provided me more time to help with the children. It also provided me more time to develop my new career and earn the respect of the new people in my life. In some ways, upon reflection, it seemed as if I was a person who had been given only a short time to live, only to find out that the prognosis was better than anticipated and more time was available. Other than my occasional slips into gloom, I was very grateful for the additional time and wanted to make the best of it.

To me, my upcoming prison stay was a bit like a death sentence. It was the bottom of the barrel for me. So, any time given to enjoy freedom was a precious gift, not to be wasted by the small stuff. Yet not a day went by that I didn't realize that I must soon face the consequences for my choices. I couldn't avoid the outcome, whatever that outcome might be.

"Okay, I'm up. Merry Christmas, Son. I love you." I jolted out of my thoughts and joined both of my sons for what would turn out to be our last Christmas together before my time in prison.

During those three years, I became a "farmer" of sorts. I didn't take up farming in the true sense. Rather, I began planting seeds that

I hoped would provide a harvest someday. If it was true that you reap what you sow, then in my mind, sowing the right seeds was important so that when the harvest came the crop would be outstanding.

All too often, people like me await an outcome, become immobilized, and forget about what they can do in the meantime. Their fear of the future is so great that it paralyzes their present experience. When the future arises, we don't always get to choose the outcome. Hence, when the outcome arrives and we find it is less than we desired, we tend to blame others, our environment, or anything other than ourselves and our choices.

I won't try to share every choice I made during this temporary "get out of jail" card. Yet, many times today, I am asked about how I recovered from the effects of my choices. After all, most convicted felons would never be able to serve in a senior management capacity with a public company.

The answer is simple—the choices I made.

During those three years, I was focused on the choices. Much to my surprise, I was given the opportunity to work, and work I did. Not only did I serve in an accounting capacity with the company that hired me, but they asked me to become involved in sales. I jumped at the opportunity.

If you're a doctor, and you violate your oaths and lose your license, you still have those skills you were taught, but it is hard to regain the trust of those who would use your skills. Perhaps applying your abilities to another endeavor would be more effective. Likewise, if you're an attorney who has been disbarred for unethical conduct, your knowledge of the law hasn't changed, but the willingness of others to secure your service may be hampered. After all, how can you help them with their legal issues if you can't operate within the law yourself?

My case was no different. I could have fought to stay in accounting, but my instinct said to move into another career. Start over. Make better choices.

The sales profession is one of the few that is a bit forgiving. First, everything has to be sold, in some form or another. Second, with few exceptions, there are no professional standards or requirements that serve as a barrier to entry into the profession. And, third, those with natural talent in sales can always find some organization that has a need and will give them a chance. Within the scope of less than eighteen months from my exit as a CPA, I found myself in sales. What a godsend.

I get odd comments from people when this part of my past enters the discussion. Some equate my entry into sales and my legal status as evidence that only scum-of-the-earth lowlifes enter into sales. How completely wrong! I have met and been mentored by some of the most professional and ethical people I know in the sales arena. To judge all salespeople as less than ethical is to judge all women by the standards that famous female pop stars have set.

What I have learned is that regardless of my past, I can accomplish anything as long as I want to make the right choices going forward. My choice of work or income wasn't the only choice that could yield the consequence that likely I desired. Every choice I made contributed to the outcome I desired.

During this same time, I focused all my income-producing efforts into making restitution. The courses I taught funded a significant part of the restitution made. Beyond that, my income from work funded the rest. All my income, excluding $700 per month, went to restitution.

Fortunately, my employer was willing to provide me a place to live. From everything I've experienced personally and have seen in the years following my incarceration, if you take the initiative to make the right choices, eventually things will come together to support your efforts and choices.

All too often, when the cards are stacked against you, when you feel that nothing is working for your good, you focus on the negative and expect the worst. What you expect, you'll likely receive. Often, it becomes a self-fulfilling prophecy. You don't make the choices you should. You quit making good choices when you don't see an immediate outcome or the outcome you want when you want it. Either way, failure to make good choices, or ceasing to make those good choices too soon, typically results in less than stellar results. People often quit moving forward just before their miracle happens, and they miss the opportunity.

> People often quit moving forward just before their
> miracle happens, and they miss the opportunity.

Some believe there's no such thing as luck. Actually, those people who seem to be lucky are the same people who also focus on making choices to support the outcome they seek. In my case, I can resoundingly say that I was not lucky. Rather, things came together for a positive outcome because I was unwilling to make choices to support anything other than the best for my family and myself.

During question-and-answer sessions after presentations, I'm often asked about making good choices for my family. I love my family and know that if I had any chance at being an effective role model for my children, the choices I made would be critical. However, the truth is, my choices were first made for me. If I did not have enough concern for myself, enough self-respect, then external motivations would be short-lived. When others come forward and ask what they could do to gain better outcomes, the first thought that comes to my mind is to care enough about yourself to want a better outcome first for you.

Time seemed to pass quickly during the three years leading up to that Christmas morning. Frankly, I knew in the back of my mind that the three years the federal government had given me had passed. In fact, by that Christmas, the three years had come and gone with no word from my attorney or the U.S. attorney. Could it be that I was to receive the greatest Christmas present I could imagine—that they had just forgotten about me?

The day had come and gone and the time with my children was precious. There's nothing like the unconditional love of a child to bring joy. When those little boys would run and jump into my arms squealing with laughter, I could not imagine not being with them. Punishment was something I dealt myself daily as I considered the possibility of what would happen, should I be taken from them through incarceration.

December 26, 1994, was a Monday. What happens on December 26 most of the time? Unless that day falls on a Sunday, the mail is delivered.

The day before, Christmas day, and a Sunday, was glorious. As I arrived home from work on Monday, I had mail from the U.S. attorney's office. They had not forgotten, not at all. The wheels of justice may move slowly, but they always come around. The three years had passed since I was given a deferred prosecution offer by the U.S. Attorney. Now that the deadline had come, I had to uphold my end of the bargain. Now was the time for me to plead guilty.

The emotional high experienced earlier was followed by an emotional low. It was familiar territory for me. I had hoped that somehow I had been forgotten in all the other issues they dealt with. My deluded desire for governmental forgetfulness was rudely burst by a very unemotional letter giving me a date and time to report to the federal courthouse to enter my guilty pleas. I walked into my home with my head even lower. The time for me to face the legal punishment phase of my consequences loomed. I just didn't know how I could walk through the doors into prison.

Punishment takes many forms. I began creating my consequences and punishment the day I made the choice to steal money from my trusting client. I've been living those consequences since that time. I felt punishment every time I looked into my wife's eyes, knowing that our relationship would never be the same. At this point, however, punishment was legal and inflicted by the government. Punishment isn't always exacted by outside forces. It is often more severe from our internal feelings, feelings of guilt or worthlessness, feelings that can gnaw at us which are more powerful that what any government can dish out. They become your internal prison, a prison worse than any governmental agency can impose upon you.

I know so well the feeling of "out of sight, out of mind." That's exactly what I was hoping for, but the reality is, you can never avoid the consequences of your actions. This letter was a very clear reminder to me of that fact. While not a day went by that I didn't think about this day, as time passed, I became more hopeful that somehow my good choices would make this nightmare go away. No such luck. Remember, you do reap what you sow, and I could not avoid the reaping. The only thing that had truly happened is that the reaping was postponed so that I would have time to sow some good seeds.

I remember walking up the steps to the federal courthouse side by side with my attorney as the day arrived for my first time before a judge. I was silent—unusual for me. I've never stood before a judge, and I felt a little overwhelmed at that prospect. I was completely willing to plead guilty to crimes I had committed. I could not argue that I did not commit them. Everyone knew I did. Having made restitution and admitting wrongdoing, I could do nothing other than plead guilty.

My hope was that the seeds I had sown during my time of freedom, along with the character witnesses, would prove to be enough to gain me a probationary sentence. After all, restitution, employment, and young children, along with exemplary character comments, should count for something. What would putting me in prison do, other than hurt others?

I had no idea what to expect. First, I was processed, fingerprinted, and photographed. Shortly thereafter, I was reunited with my attorney as I stepped nervously into the courtroom. I had been in a courtroom before, but then I had been on the jury. I admit, it was fun then, when I was not the one on trial. Although there was no jury for me—I was just there to plead guilty—I still found it very uncomfortable, knowing that whatever was to happen with me was happening now.

"How do you plead?" was the judge's question to my attorney and me.

"Guilty, your honor," responded my attorney.

"To both counts, counselor?"

"Yes, your honor. My client pleads guilty to both counts."

The time spent there was fairly short, with the judge accepting my plea and indicating sentencing would follow. I walked into the court a free man and walked out a convicted felon. Never in my wildest dreams would I have thought that my time in a courtroom would be focused on my actions.

As I walked out of the courtroom, my attorney set the stage for things to come. He let me know that sentencing would likely be several months away, and that in the meantime, I needed to make sure I didn't get in further trouble with the law. His last admonishment was a nonissue, as I had changed my behavior and become more honest and real with myself over the past four years. Frankly, I was hoping that the positive choices I had made would keep me out of prison. Probation I could handle—prison, well, that was another issue; one that I did not want to face.

How many of us truly want to face the demons we've created and the consequences before us? Whether it is issues with substance abuse, relationship issues, abuse issues, or a host of other prisons we often find ourselves in, I doubt that many of us find joy in facing the outcome head on. Rather, it's much easier to revert to old ways, comfortable ways, and hope that the future consequence never arrives.

Like most, after the conviction was over, I began my day-to-day routines. I believed that somehow I could avoid the likelihood of prison, if only I lived an exemplary life. Surely the judge would see what I had done, and find it in his heart to show what I thought would be well deserved mercy.

In early June, 1995, I had just finished an extensive recruiting session and started a training class for my employer. One thing I dearly enjoyed was the opportunity to train. By now, the opportunity to speak had passed, as most of my former clients had been absorbed by other presenters. It's hard to be effective as a presenter to CPAs when you've lost your license and been convicted for what is abhorrent to the profession. So, in-house training was the only practical outlet for my talents and the best way to recapture the joy of presenting.

As the first day of training ended, I was interrupted by Betty, one of the most caring administrative assistants I've had the privilege of working with.

"Chuck, you've got a call up at the office," she announced as she walked into the training room.

"Take a message, please," I replied. One thing that really bugged me was interruptions in training, and while I loved Betty, she wasn't allowed to interrupt, either.

"It's your attorney, and he said he'd hold!" And with that said, Betty walked out.

"Excuse me. I'll be back in a few," I told the class as I made my way up to the office. Thinking all the way there, I had concluded that Betty and I had to have a talk. Surely she could have been more discreet. Saying your attorney is on the line in front of a class of new trainees was just inexcusable. I suspected that she did that so that I would confide in her what was going on. As it was, I had shared with no one my background, conviction, or possible future. If my future included probation, as I saw it, there was no need to reveal my sordid past. I almost think it was easier to focus my attention on Betty than to wonder what my attorney would have to say.

Perhaps he's calling to tell me that my sentencing is probation. That thought was pressing on my mind as I took those three steps up to the office door. Pulling the noisy screen door open, Betty caught my eye and pointed to the phone with three fingers raised. That meant line three.

By the way she looked at me and pointed to the phone, I got the feeling that she expected me to take it right there, in an open office, so that all could hear—especially Betty! No such luck. Looking down the hall for an open office, I closed the door and stared at the phone for a moment. Usually I would jump at the chance to talk, but frankly, I wasn't sure this was a call that I really wanted to take.

"Chuck, Frank here. Your hearing is set for tomorrow morning at 10:00 a.m. You need to be there with any character witnesses you might have. I'll meet you at the courthouse."

"Frank, I've just started a training class. Can't we postpone this for a week?"

"Chuck, it is tomorrow."

He had warned me that it would likely be early June, but I expected a little more warning. As I said, my attorney was a man of few words. I was hoping that luck would fall my way, but I received very little encouragement from Frank. He was straight to the point and practical with his advice. Somehow I think his parents did the right thing by naming him because his approach was defined by his name.

As I stepped out of the door from the office where I took the call, I remember hearing, as if in the distance somewhere, Betty say, "Chuck, are you all right?" I have no clue what my response was. In that moment I began to feel the weight of all my past deeds weigh heavy on my shoulders, if not on my very being. I felt as if I were in a fog and couldn't connect to the present moment.

> One word uttered from the mouth of
> someone who didn't know me—"prison" or
> "probation"—would define my future.

Reality began to sink in as I walked back down the hill to my new training class. I felt the anxious fear in the pit of my stomach. Tomorrow, I would face my fate. One word uttered from the mouth of someone who didn't know me—"prison" or "probation"—would define my future. With that thought in my head, it was hard for me to focus on the class.

"Ladies and gentlemen, I'm so sorry, but tomorrow I have to be out of town. There is nothing worse than dealing with attorneys on their time frame." And with those words out of my mouth, I tried to edge out a smile as if everything was all right. How would they know otherwise?

"We'll pick back up on Wednesday," I said, and with that I dismissed the group. Would I be back on Wednesday? Frankly, by that point, my mind was racing with all that had to be done to corral the folks who had agreed to testify on my behalf. Stilling an active mind is hard, especially when you think that actions can manipulate consequences. For my part, the idea of garnering the troops to appear on my behalf was my last desperate effort to bring about a "probation" outcome.

Even in June, there was a crispness in the early morning air in Asheville, North Carolina, as we arrived well over an hour early. I had hoped this day would never arrive, that somehow the government would see all that I had done to correct my past misdeeds, that somehow it all would be a bad dream, and that I would wake up to the comfort of knowing that it was over. Thoughts like that are unrealistic. We can't escape the outcome that most surely will follow our actions. And, today, with time to ponder, I entered the outer area of the federal courthouse with nothing to do but wait for my character witnesses and attorney to arrive. Wait and think—that was all that was left to do.

I felt as if I could be watching a Perry Mason episode, except I was watching myself as the central character. There I was, with my attorney behind the enormous wooden table hearing, "All rise." I couldn't begin to tell you what else was said. The official seemed to be speaking in a foreign language. "Be seated!" And with that, the process began.

I found myself in amazement at the speed of the process. My character witnesses were questioned but not given the time I thought they needed to share the truth about my exemplary behavior and the truth about why I should receive probation. All seemed rote, as if the parties were going through the motions but with no concern or emotion. Even the judge acted somewhat disinterested. It was as if the decision were already made and they only had to go through the motions to appease the law. They were talking about my life, my freedom. I wanted so badly to make an emotional plea for compassionate clemency. After all, how could justice rule with any other verdict other than "probation?"

As the judge began to speak, I have no recollection of anything he said, other than "eighteen months active, three years supervised release." This couldn't be. Had he not heard all the facts of the case, my character witnesses? Could he not see how much I had changed and how remorseful I was regarding my initial choices? I wanted to scream at him, but I just stood there silent and in shock. This couldn't be happening.

> The gavel dropped, and the party was over. I had just
> been sentenced to an active prison sentence.

The gavel dropped, and the party was over. I had just been sentenced to an active prison sentence. One phase of this nightmare was over and the next phase had yet to begin. How could this be?

In disbelief, I followed my attorney out of the courtroom and took his instructions regarding what to do next. Perhaps it was because of the crime, perhaps it was because of my behavior—I don't know—but I was not escorted out like a common criminal. Rather, I was given my freedom without bond. I was told that I would be given a date to report to prison, but no time frame was given, and I was left once again to wonder when that date would be.

Within forty-five minutes of the hearing beginning, I was back on the road to my home. The trip back seemed like an eternity, and I doubt twenty-five words were spoken, at least by me. I had withdrawn into my own little world, facing once again an unknown future. I really believed that the one thing I was sure I would avoid by all my right actions was going to prison. It was the one thing I feared and the one thing I would have to face completely and totally alone. No one could help me in prison. There I would be alone, with time on my hands to deal with the thoughts of my deeds and the reality I had created for myself. There would be no way to avoid looking at the truth of what I had done and what I had become. What I couldn't see at that moment was the opportunity to truly change my future. This step was necessary to secure my journey forward.

As evening dawned, I went into my apartment, wishing that the day I had just experienced had never happened. I had held my emotions in check. That night, as I turned on some music to calm my tattered emotions, a song that came on touched a chord. For the first time in a long time, I sobbed. I was feeling the remorse for five years of earlier actions that seemed insignificant at the time, but were proving to be pivotal for me now. Every choice has a consequence, and my choices had come full circle, shattering my former self. Perhaps that had to happen so I could accomplish what my mother told me so many times when she said, "Son, you can be somebody!" Perhaps I had to face this time alone to come to understand I was somebody.

"Shattered," a song by Jimmy Webb, played when the emotion flood gate opened. "Shattered, like a windowpane, broken by a stone; each tiny piece of me lies alone." I heard those words and others that followed. I was shattered, at least for the moment. But this too will pass, I thought, as the tears flowed like rain.

10

Next Steps—The Day After

---◆---

"I've got to admit, I admire what you've done. I think if it had been me, the day after being sentenced to prison, I would have hopped a flight to Mexico and left it all behind."

Those comments, made a month after my sentencing, seemed foreign to me. I appreciated what the regional president of the company said, but the thoughts he expressed had never crossed my mind. While it was painful being sentenced to prison, the person I had become was far different from the person I was some five short years earlier. In five years, I had grown through the experience. While the journey had not been easy, it was a journey where I was forced to face myself. Running away would only prolong the outcome, not circumvent it. More importantly, it would just about undo everything I had accomplished during the past few years.

More times than not, through a lot of reflection, I did not like what I saw in the mirror staring back at me. The defects of character I exhibited were repulsive. I wasn't very forgiving of myself, and the system was not so forgiving either. The sentence could not equal the self-debasement I lived with every day. I knew better than to do what I did so many years earlier, and at times I wondered how I had ever made such a poor mistake. What was wrong with me that would allow me to choose to do something obviously wrong?

In the trial by fire, I came quickly to understand that, although I thought I was invincible, the reality was that I was not in control. God, or a universal power, had my life in divine order. I had confused reality and the consequences that always follow our choices. Coming to that understanding, and feeling the pain that comes from the consequences of poor choices, were enough for me to understand that I had to make better choices.

The day after I was sentenced to prison was a struggle. What was I going to do? My energy felt drained, and I was challenged to gain the momentum to move forward—with anything. A part of me wanted to stay in bed and wallow in my self-pity. Part of me wondered what the use was of moving forward with the day. After all, I was going to prison, and it wouldn't matter what I did anymore. As I looked in the mirror that morning, I knew that today would be a defining moment in my life. Today I had a choice, and it made sense to me that I needed to make the most of what lay ahead. If choices could produce negative consequences, they could also produce positive results. So I didn't get what I wanted with probation. I still had my freedom today, and today I could choose how to respond in a positive way and receive positive results. God knew that I needed some positive results in my life. To receive them, all I had to do was walk fully aware into this day.

> If choices could produce negative consequences,
> they could also produce positive results.

Up to this point, every good experience happened when I peeled back the veil of illusion and became brutally honest with myself and those around me. As I stood in the shower, I felt bathed with the understanding that today was no different. While my superiors knew of the struggles I had been facing, and those I had to face yet, the people I worked with knew nothing of them. They knew what they saw in me, not the truth of all of me. They did not know the complete reality of who I was that day. Today was the day to share with all the real Chuck Gallagher. With every fiber of my being, I knew that if I were to move forward in a positive way, today I had to bare all, share all, and step forward in faith. If there were truth to the phrase "you reap what you sow," then perhaps sowing seeds of honesty would produce a harvest of compassion, love, and, eventually, joy. I didn't want to live with the illusion anymore. The responsibility was too great. Today the illusion would die, regardless of the consequences.

As I stepped through the door, I asked Betty if she would contact the staff and ask them to gather for a special meeting at 10:00 a.m.

"What's it about?" she asked with a playful grin on her face.

"You'll know when you get there. Can you call them now? If they are serving a customer, I'll understand their absence." Her facial expression changed immediately. She, like most people in a corporate environment, suspected the worst. I knew that with no one knowing what was to come, I would certainly have record attendance at this impromptu meeting.

It was funny but, two days before, I was "in charge" to those who worked with and for me. Today, however, would be dramatically different. Today would be shocking for some and humbling for me. It's not easy to peel back the layers of ego and reveal the sometimes brutal truth.

I began to wonder what my co-workers' response would be. I was not looking for sympathy or pity. Like so often in my past, the time had come to remove the illusion with these co-workers. For too long, the illusion had taken too much of my energy—energy that would be better invested in sowing good seeds. So few realize what an energy thief maintaining an illusion can be. The time had arrived when I needed to reveal the truth and let the chips fall wherever they landed. There was some relief in knowing that perhaps by sharing the true nature, I would be free to be who I really was and not the illusion of what people thought they knew about me. Somehow that seemed freeing to me and yet unnerving at the same time.

It's kind of funny to watch the process of people gathering for a "called" meeting when they have no clue what the subject is; the comments and rumors that grow are simply amazing. Some speculated that we were announcing the company being sold, while others just knew that someone was seriously ill. Strange, but no one speculated that something good might be happening. Guess that's human nature.

"Thank you for gathering here on such short notice," I began. This was my first time to publicly admit my past and, while speaking was never a real issue for me, today it felt dramatically different. Today this group of people would meet the real Chuck Gallagher.

"Yesterday, I had to make a trip to the western part of the state. This was a trip that I dreaded, but one that had to be made. You see, many years ago—nine, in fact—I made a choice that has proved to be life changing."

I explained my choices and the consequences that followed. Having resolved to be totally honest, I held nothing back; nothing was sugarcoated or portrayed in a way that painted me as anything other than a liar and a thief. Those were brutal facts. While I was not and am not proud of that reality, it nonetheless remains a fact of my past. I concluded, "As a result of those fateful choices, yesterday I was sentenced to federal prison."

Even today, I can still see the faces of the people sitting there. At first, there was complete silence. I expected harsh judgment and got none. Some sat in disbelief with tears streaming down their faces, stunned by the truth. Others wanted to fight, feeling that something was wrong with the system. After all, I had made restitution and changed my life. How could this be justice? Others reached out, offering their kind of love, whatever form that took.

What I recall most as those final words were spoken was an overwhelming feeling of compassionate love. People had a choice.

They could accept me with all my imperfections or reject me. Either way, the admission of my wrongs in an honest, public way proved cathartic. I was going to prison, but I was freer than most.

"Does anyone here have any questions?" It never really crossed my mind that I would have a "question and answer" session about going to prison, but I felt that the more they knew, the quicker we could all go on with our lives. My objective was not to be a disruption.

"When will you go to prison?" one asked.

"I don't know," I responded. "I was told they will let me know when they are ready." Then, with what little humor I could muster, I stated, "You know, I'm not in any rush to get there!"

The questions didn't last long. As the meeting was starting to break up, I ended with one last comment. "I know today has been unexpected. For those of you who are in training: if you don't mind, I'd like to take the rest of the day off to give both you and me some time to reflect. If you don't wish to come back and complete your training, since you now know you'll be trained by a convicted felon, I understand. Otherwise, we will resume training tomorrow at 9:00 a.m. Meeting adjourned."

I left, both exhausted and energized. No longer would I have to maintain the illusion of perfection. I could manage each day, now knowing that I didn't need to hide anymore.

That day was a defining moment for me. I was a free man with freedom to choose. I would endure physical imprisonment, but my soul would be free. I earned my prison sentence with my choices, but I would enter and serve my prison sentence as a free man.

The following day was training as usual, as was the day after that, and every day following. In fact, other than spending time with my children, I worked every day up until the time I reported for prison.

11

On the 24th Step, I . . .

On the twenty-third step, I looked back one last time, not sure what I was looking for—perhaps some miraculous reprieve. There was nothing there. With my next step, the twenty-fourth step, I extended my right hand, opened the door, and stepped into federal prison.

I looked forward as I entered and saw only the prison officials. This was my life ahead of me. At that moment, I was filled with the strength to go forward that could only come from God's love. In the presence of my best friend, the prison officials treated me kindly. I would soon learn that kindness would fade quickly. My belongings were searched and then transferred from the small cloth suitcase I brought to a plastic garbage bag. Saying goodbye, I choked back tears. I wanted to be strong for my friend, and I am sure she for me, neither of us really believing. With goodbyes said, she turned to leave, as did I. She walked back into freedom, and I entered the dark world of prison.

Every step was a new experience. I was almost like a baby. Sure, I was in a man's body and acted accordingly, but like a baby, I was led each step of the way. I had to trust that where or how I was being led was going to be all right. I did as I was told. I wasn't sure what the alternative would be, and I had no intention of finding out.

Immediately after arrival, as the guards prepared for lunch, my trash bag of possessions was taken from me, and I was placed in a locked cinder block cell probably no larger than eight-foot by ten-foot. There was a wooden bench to sit on and a ceramic toilet. Beyond that, it was isolation in a sterile environment. This was a far cry from what I had ten years ago, even from what I had yesterday.

With a sick feeling in the pit of my stomach, I looked around, and I realized that my life now was not my own. My choices some ten years ago had brought me to an unimaginable place. Never in my wildest dreams would I have ever guessed, even with remote speculation, that I would be here, in prison.

How many people in their lives, facing dire consequences, have the same questions? How did I get here? What was I thinking? Somehow, the reality of negative consequences has the ability to clarify our vision, thoughts, and actions. Unfortunately, as humans, we don't have that clarity of vision at the time the choices are being made. If we did, most certainly there would be far fewer negative consequences. Perhaps our growth comes from learning the lessons we encounter through our choices.

I was offered lunch, but refused. This had been my last morning of freedom, so I exercised my right to eat what I wanted and how much I wanted. Hunger was not at the top of my list of concerns. It was difficult enough sitting in that cell that first day. Waves of anxiety flowed through me, challenging that big breakfast to stay down. No, more food was not what I needed. I needed my freedom. I needed to be able to get up and walk out of those doors using my free will.

So I was left there—just a wooden bench, a toilet, and me. I had never been locked anywhere unless it was my choosing, but not this day. There I sat, awash with a flood of memories. Time passed slowly. I went back as I sat there, way back, trying to put this all into perspective, recalling, understanding, and discovering what had set this all up so long ago.

I was lost in my own thoughts, not knowing how much time had passed. Startled by the sound of keys in the door, I heard a guard open the door and order me to step outside for processing. The three hours of reflection in a holding cell had ended, and the journey into a frightening new world began. As I exited, I was faced with a man in a white lab coat by the name of Pedro. He was a physician's assistant, and he had first crack at us as we moved through the processing sequence. Beside me were two other men: an African-American man, large in stature with a huge gold front tooth, and a Hispanic man who had tattoos covering most of his visible body.

After we lined up, Pedro stated with a heavy Hispanic accent, "It's time for your TB test." He produced a four-pronged needle used to administer the test. Just the thought of a needle causes my blood pressure to fall, and I feel faint. So here I am, my first time in prison, accompanied by two other inmates, and I'm facing one of my worst fears—a simple needle.

"Roll up your sleeves," Pedro commanded. Then he looked at me. "You first!"

I rolled up my sleeve and extended my arm. I thought, "Be cool, Chuck. You can make it through a simple TB test. It's no big deal." As the needle pricked my skin on the inside of my left arm, the sensation began to hit. Then the cold sweat began to break out on my forehead. Pedro looked at me. "You okay?"

"I need to sit down."

Without a moments notice, Pedro yelled to the guard at the door, "We've got a fainter!"

As I maneuvered to a wooden bench nearby, I quickly sat and placed my head between my knees, trying to regain my composure. I couldn't get it out of my mind. *Here it is, my first day in prison, and I'm about to pass out. What kind of image will this leave for the other two standing here? I really don't want to be someone's wife.* Obviously, I had watched way too much TV, and fear was overtaking rationality in my thoughts.

Then I heard an unexpected voice. The African-American inmate looked at me. Strange, but I could see compassion in his eyes. In any other setting I could imagine that he would tear me apart with his strength, but here we were the same. "Yo, man, it's all right. None of us want to be here. You'll be okay."

We could choose to claim those barriers that divide so many, or we could look past them and know that we were all in this together.

With his words, I began to recover from my fear of needles. Somehow, in his own way, he reached out, looking past the illusion that I saw. He understood a simple truth—we were all facing the consequences of our choices. None of us liked the consequences we were facing, and each of us would have to deal with it in his own way. The one thing we had in common was each other. We could choose to claim those barriers that divide so many, or we could look past them and know that we were all in this together.

While the three of us were assigned to different areas of the prison facility after processing, when our paths crossed from time to time, there was an unspoken bond that existed. All it took was a look and a nod of the head to know.

By 3:25 p.m., I had been fully processed and was escorted to my cell, my new home. As I entered the cell, my cell mate, Buck, an African-American man of mid-stature, walked out. He gave me a quick once-over, never uttering a word. By this time, I had been instructed to change into my prison uniform and be prepared for "count time" at 4:00 p.m. I guess that meant something to most people, but it didn't connect with me. Doing as I was told, I changed and sat on the bed assigned, waiting for further instructions.

At three minutes to 4:00 p.m., Buck reentered the cell. He just looked at me again—sizing me up, I suppose. Then a noise broke the chatter of inmates in this area.

"Count time. Count time."

Again, Buck looked at me, pointing at the floor as if I knew what to do. I stood up just as the guard passed by our cell, counting each inmate as we stood in silence. I watched others, waiting for a cue as to what to do next. When the count was done, the chatter began, and once again, Buck left the room with no comments.

Seated on my excuse for a bed, I began to drift into a contemplative state. Now disconnected from all that I knew, all that was familiar, I was preparing to enter a part of life that would prove to be painful. And yet, it was an opportunity for accelerated growth. We all have thoughts, beliefs, and associations; we interpret and make judgments. I did not, at that moment, think of prison as a place for growth; rather, it was a place of dread, a place to be endured. I would assume that most people feel that the consequences they face, especially if they judge them to be negative consequences, are unwanted and carry no benefit other than pain. Yet, through experience—my own as well as what is reported by others—often the worst experiences we face are our greatest teachers if we are open to allowing the lesson.

As the first night began to pass, I can't say my first day in prison was fraught with any danger. I was just a number. I was another person placed somewhere where he didn't want to be, dealing with the internal issues of doing time for something and learning in a new and unfamiliar environment. Staring at the ceiling of the cell and trying to get warm under the prison-issued sheet and blanket, I wondered if there was ever a time when the choices I made were worth the price. My eyes welling with tears, but crying my first night was not an option.

Before the crack of dawn on day two, the guards banged on the door to the unit and began flashing on the lights. Buck was immediately out of bed as the workday began. I, on the other hand, was bewildered. I suppose I expected prison to be a place where you stayed in your bed until you wanted to get up, did nothing, and did nothing some more.

Buck looked up at me, as I was on the top bunk.

"You better get up and get out of here before 8:00 a.m. or the 'hacks' will put you to work." With those words, Buck was off to his job. It was 6:45 a.m.

Well, he talks, I thought to myself, not knowing what to do. Just then, the silence was broken. Another inmate, a middle-aged guy, poked his head around the corner.

"You eat?" he asked with a tentative look on his face, as if he might have disturbed me. "Your first day here?"

"Yeah," I replied, honestly glad to have someone who showed some interest. Not that I expected a welcoming party, but rarely had I ever been somewhere where you were looked right through, as if you were nobody. Perhaps it was learned behavior, but even in the "projects," people seemed to have some basic level of respect and concern. Yet, except for the African-American guy from yesterday, no one seemed to care. Well, not until now.

"I'm Ham."

"Chuck," I replied. He offered no hand, and neither did I. I had already made up my mind that I would observe and take my lead from others who had been here awhile. I did not know the ropes, and being a leader in prison was not something I had ever aspired to.

"Follow me. Let's get some breakfast." With that, Ham moved out, expecting me to follow. "Now, don't expect much. You know, the inmates do the cooking around here. The breakfast bunch, well, they ain't the best. The dinner cooks, well, that's another story. They're pretty good. We'll get some good chow at night."

Have you ever been around someone who just won't shut up? Ham was that type. I guess he needed someone to talk to as well, and I was new. The feeling was one of conflict. On one hand, I felt intense appreciation for the kindness Ham offered to me by showing me the ropes on my first morning there. On the other hand, his non-stop chatter annoyed me. Quiet reflection seemed to be more important to me at the time. Before I ever took those twenty-three steps, I had made a personal commitment to keep a journal of the experience. I was conscious enough to know that there would be something positive to come from what, on the surface, appeared to be an extremely bad situation. Perhaps the entries into the journal would be helpful.

Fortunately, Ham had to go to work as well. Due to his age, likely mid-60s, he had a job on the prison grounds. As we left the "chow" hall, Ham cautioned, "Don't go back to the unit. Go to the library or something. Otherwise, they'll put you to work." Ham went on his way as he pointed the way to a place for me to write.

Looking back at those journal entries I wrote so many years ago brings back a flood of memories. Somehow, on that first day I seemed to have a stream of consciousness flow through my fingers. I penned fourteen pages. Thoughts, feelings, guilt from past actions, all just flowed as I lost track of time immersed in writing.

Startled by a loud horn sounding, I noticed that inmates that surrounded me were getting up and moving back to their units, so I followed suit. Feeling a gnawing in my stomach, I became aware that now for the second day in a row I had missed lunch. I became so caught up in writing that I forgot to eat lunch, and one thing I found quickly in prison was that you eat what they tell you, when they tell you, or you go without. Unlike places I had been in the past, I couldn't go to a fast food joint and grab a quick bite or stop at a convenience store. The prison had its rules and we were there to abide by them.

Perhaps this was another aspect of learning. Often, the recognition that there is an authority more powerful than you is a revelation to some, especially to those of us who seemed to think that our choices were above and beyond consequences. We were facing the direct consequences of our choices and, as I was beginning to quickly ascertain, those who ran the prison were there to make sure we knew that. Their job, in part, was to make sure that we understood that we no longer had any control over our lives.

> Often, the recognition that there is an authority more powerful than you is a revelation to some, especially to those of us who seemed to think that our choices were above and beyond consequences.

The process of learning is different for each person. Often, before entering prison, I had wondered why this was happening. Why did it have to come to this? After all, I had paid so much already. I felt frustrated and angry for a moment. I admitted my crime, made amends and restitution, and changed my path. Prison was unnecessary. Or was it? Maybe the complete and total loss of control was the consequence that was needed to make sure that the lesson was learned. Maybe the answer lay hidden here somewhere.

Sitting on my bed, just as Buck had left me, is exactly how he found me as he reentered the cell from his workday. "What's up," I asked as he came in, thinking that I'd break the silence that was so deafening on the first day. I figured that the worst thing that would happen was that he wouldn't reply.

"What's you in here for, anyhow," he asked with a black man's brogue, which I can hear but can't spell. For a moment I thought to myself, *What should I reply? I can't come across as weak. I've never been in this situation before.* So, with my toughest look—which I can imagine wasn't very tough—I replied.

"I'm a thief."

"Word?"

Looking back at Buck, I didn't have a clue what he said. So I did the only thing I knew to do. I repeated what I heard. "Word?"

"Yo man, word?"

With what must have been a serious, puzzled look, Buck then said to me, "You don't have a clue what I'm saying—dooze ya?" And with that, he turned and flew out of the cell as if in a rush to get somewhere.

With such crystal clarity, I recall my thoughts as if today were that same second day in prison. *What just happened?* I thought to myself. *Wow, if this is what this is going to be like, this is going to be a hard time.* And, just as soon as those thoughts cleared my mind, Buck rushed back in.

Buck's eyes were dark chocolate, and they had a piercing kind of intensity. Looking me over from top to bottom, Buck uttered an offer that changed the course of my experience in prison. Just a shade more than twenty-four hours had passed, and little did I know that the power of a lesson would come so quickly.

"I'll makes ya a deal," Buck said to me with his piercing stare.

Wondering what in the world Buck had on his mind, I thought, *Here is a guy who I have just met. He hasn't spoken twenty words to me, yet now he's interested in making me a 'deal.'*

He spoke up. "You won't make it in here. You don't know the lingo. You'd never make it in the hood."

At that moment, I knew Buck was right. I was a fish out of water, and it didn't take him long to know it. I had tried hard not to be obvious, but a well-spoken white guy surrounded by mostly gang members and drug dealers must stand out.

"I'll have your back and teach you the lingo, if you'll teach me how to speak properly so that I have a chance at getting a real job when I get out of here!"

As he spoke those words, he extended his hand in friendship.

While there were many more days to follow, let me say, Buck kept his word. He taught me the lingo. He taught me how to survive in prison and, likely, in the "hood." Likewise, I did my part. Not only did I teach him to speak, but I helped Buck get his first job when he obtained his freedom from prison.

Buck was an angel to me in prison. He began a lesson that I have never forgotten. He taught me the real meaning of success, not defined by the illusion that surrounds us, but rather, by the impact that we have on other people's lives.

Buck's impact on me was profound. He had more integrity than most of the people I had done business with so many years before. Here we were, judged by most to be the lowest of the low, and yet, even in an environment like prison, Buck was able to live successfully. Denied the trappings of societal success, prison is a fertile learning lab for understanding and living the values of real success. For that, I am ever thankful.

The lessons did not stop with survival in prison. There were so many more lessons to be gained. Many months had passed since that day with Buck at the beginning of my prison journey. I learned how to fit in and even began to work. We were all there for different crimes, and each of our experiences was unique. We lived with our own private pains.

12

Christmas Memories and a Three-Minute Call

---◆---

On Christmas morning, my first and, as I thought, hopefully my last in prison, I lay in my bed feeling an aching in my chest. The pain was not from a physical ailment. Rather, the pain was an emotional ache that hurt to the very core of my soul, perhaps more deeply than any physical pain I ever experienced before. Although Christmas was my favorite time of year, this year it was the most painful time, and I was not alone in those thoughts. By this time, Buck and I had developed a close bond. Even he found Christmas morning difficult, and he had seen six of them come and go before I got there. I couldn't imagine what that was like.

Five hundred men in this prison facility and on Christmas day, most of them would shed a tear. Being in prison doesn't make anyone immune from pain and loss. On days like today, it magnifies the pain and loss. Just like them, as I lay motionless in my top bunk bed, I found myself thinking with tears streaming down my face. I cannot, to this day, say why the thought came to mind, but it made a powerful impression. It seemed that this "learning laboratory" had the tendency to teach at a rapid rate. At least, it did for me.

I recalled one evening, sometime back in the mid-eighties, standing in the checkout line at the grocery store I frequented in my former hometown. At that time, I was in my mid to late twenties and had a budding career. Now, I must admit, I thought that was an odd thing to recall on Christmas morning in prison, but this is what came to mind. Looking back, there was clearly a reason.

The memory was crystal clear. I had walked into the store quickly to buy some steak and shrimp, having told my wife I would pick up some on my way home. We were to grill out that night, and I knew it would save her a trip. Little did I know that something so simple would provide such a profound lesson. Frankly, I had forgotten the experience until that day—Christmas morning in 1995.

As I entered the checkout line, the clerk, a female around my age, spoke to me.

"Chuck Gallagher. You're Chuck Gallagher."

"Yes." Somewhat startled, I responded tentatively, realizing I had no idea who this person was and how she knew me. Here I was, standing in my suit, having just finished a workday at the office, and now I was being identified by a stranger at the grocery store.

"I'm Suzie," she said, as if I should know her.

I did catch her name as it was on the badge she wore on her grocery store smock. Even though she knew me, for the life of me, I had no clue who she was. Not only did I not know her name, but her face was also unfamiliar. While I tried not to show my unfamiliarity, my face must have given it away.

"We went to high school together," she exclaimed, as if that should somehow jog my memory. "I read about you often in the paper. You seem to be doing so well." Noticing my wedding ring, she then asked, "Do you have any children?"

"Yes, one," I replied, smiling at her as I acknowledged her obvious warmth. I was just trying to be nice and carry on conversation, even though inside I just wanted to check out and move on. Then I asked what, in retrospect, was a dangerous question, "Do you?" Little did I know that those simple two words would change the course of this unexpected visit.

With my question she responded, "Yes, three." And with that, she stopped the process, even though we were in the express lane. She reached under the counter, removed her pocketbook, and proceeded to take out her wallet, wherein she had two pictures each for three children—and that was just the beginning.

Standing there, I could tell that the people in line were perturbed at her for the lengthy explanation and at me for even asking. Frankly, I wasn't excited either. I didn't remember her and I was just being nice. In reality, I just wanted to get out the door and get home. As she began to wind down, I knew not to ask any further questions.

"It's so good to see you," she said as she handed me the receipt for my purchases. "Maybe we'll see each other again sometime."

I smiled and quickly walked away.

As I walked to the Mercedes I was then driving, I gloried in self-righteous thoughts. How important I was. She had read about me in the paper. I was 'somebody.' All of this time away from high school and the highest rung of the ladder she had aspired to was a check-out chick at the local grocery store. That thought was judgmental, ugly, and turned out to be profound.

Yet, on that Christmas day, 1995, as I lay on my top bunk, my thoughts drifted back to that incident. I couldn't even remember her name, yet, in my mind's eye, I vividly saw her with her family on this Christmas day.

No doubt she and her husband shared joy as their children squealed with delight over the meager gifts Santa left. Most of the time you can't get kids out of bed, but on Christmas morning they won't stay in bed. The joy and love you feel as a parent, seeing those tiny little eyes light up as they experience Christmas, is hard to describe. That feeling is one I ached to have there in prison on Christmas morning.

I imagined seeing her as she prepared their Christmas meal. As their energy began to wane, she would hold her children in her arms and tell them that she loved them. As I lay there, I imagined her gently stroking their heads as they struggled to keep their eyes open, fearing they might miss something. Gently, they would fall asleep in her arms. All those thoughts passed as I noticed the wetness of the pillow against my cheeks. She was home with her little ones. She was more of a "somebody" than I had ever dreamed of being. She was there, and I was in prison.

Monday – December 25, 1995 – Journal

Today is my 85th day in prison and surely the most miserable I will face. As the morning broke today, my two precious children arose to a warm house full of love, anxious to see what Santa left. This year is the first, however, that Daddy has not been there with them.

They are in the moment. I don't know if my absence will be significant—but it sure hurts deep in my heart. How I miss the smiles, laughter, joy, and hugs of two anxious children as they are fully engaged in unwrapping presents. I recall I used to think that getting the gift was the greatest thing. Now I know, as an adult, that more joy—much more joy—is found in sharing their joy, something that today, I can't do. Here, away from them, I can't share in that joy. This is my punishment, and I will never forget it. Never!

Funny, but today, the mood of my fellow inmates is subdued. As I look around from the vantage point of my upper bunk, I see little movement. The loud talking and cursing of the inmates is conspicuously absent. Many of the old timers seem to be sleeping the day away. They see it as just another day, one they hope will pass quickly.

Today is supposed to be the celebration of the birth of Jesus. In many ways, we have made it something else. I never really thought about how we celebrate this day until today, and looking at it from this vantage point brings some things clearly into focus. It's not the gifts; what's really important is being able to share with those that you love. How my heart aches, knowing that I rest here alone from those who I love so dearly.

Only one other time in my life do I recall pain more intense than this. But that was then and this is now. At least I know better the direction of my path and benefit of the lessons I am now learning. It's time now to make some phone calls and engage life . . .

As the thought passed, I knew there were still choices to make. I could wallow in self-pity, or make a choice that would brighten my day and perhaps the day of others. A part of me longed to continue feeling sorry for myself, but I chose to move past it. With that, I got up and stood in the phone line. Most of the time there wasn't a line for the pay phone, but today, Christmas day, there was a long one. So I waited my turn in order to make a three-minute collect call to tell my children, "Merry Christmas."

Learning and understanding is a process. Understanding comes from living, from experiencing, and from learning the lessons life's events offer you. Right action, a by-product of experience, is necessary if knowledge is to come alive. If it took me coming to prison to understand what it really means to be somebody, then it was worthwhile.

13

All Things Work for Our Good

Fourteen days short of six months in prison and the question arose: "Where from here?" Indeed, where from here? Every day is much the same as the day before. There is nothing fun about being an inmate. Having never been incarcerated, I experienced many things that I never expected to encounter. Never in my wildest dreams did I think that, while in college, I would end up in prison. I was full of optimism. Embezzlement was not at all within my mind-set, yet it became a choice I made under great stress. It's odd to look back and see the path as lessons unfold. Such a review brings up volatile emotions.

In prison, the challenges faced were not so much physical as they were mental. Around every turn, there was someone who was willing to tear me down—someone willing to cut away any of my remaining self-esteem. I came to understand that the treatment in prison was only a microcosm of what many experience in the outside world. It made me think of the homeless on the streets, where people make disgusting, demeaning comments to or about them. I thought about the person consumed in the throes of alcoholism or drug addiction. My prison experience taught me a lot about compassion towards my fellow human beings.

Many become victims of those mental challenges within the walls of prison and outside the walls of prison. For me, how I handled those struggles was completely within my control. I could become "the man's" victim, or I could choose to overcome. These are the same choices we all face in the outside world. There are always those whose chief purpose is to destroy any remnant of humanity. I chose to overcome my circumstances. My intention, when I entered prison, was to learn all the lessons available to me.

From the first day of incarceration, I wrote a journal. As I look back and read, it becomes clear that life often develops what it demands. The demand of hard times develops strong spirits, and through that comes learning.

Life often seems to get worse before it gets better; this appears to be part of the process of change.

Saturday – March 17, 1996 – Journal

I awoke this morning, as I do many mornings, in a contemplative state. One of the first things I heard was an inmate say to Buck (my cell mate), "I'm sick." Buck replied, "You're sick?" He said, "Yeah, homesick." "Me, too!" Buck said. "Me, too!"

When he came in our room, Buck asked me, "Don't you hate to wake up miserable? You know, we should wake up with joy in our hearts!" I felt deeply, hearing what he said, and replied, "I've about forgotten what that's like."

I suppose one of the eternal struggles is to find peace and joy, no matter what the situation. Personally, I think that's near impossible. Note, as an optimist, I didn't say impossible, but, at the least, it's tough, tough, tough.

You hear people claim that they've found inner joy and a peace that passes all understanding. That, I believe, comes with spiritual growth and connectedness. And I admit—I haven't reached the point where I can

118

claim that feeling always. I have felt it before, but likewise, I felt pain as I struggled to learn life's lessons.

I still find times when the loneliness of prison covers me with a wave of sadness that's hard to explain. The best description I can now give is that I once clung to life by a strong rope. Over the past several years—strand by strand—the rope has broken or become frayed such that now I'm hanging on by a mere thread. Honestly, I fear the last strand breaking and all being lost.

As I write this, however, I know that for something to be born anew, there must be a change and a cleansing. When a baby is born, there is pain, pressure, blood, discomfort, and finally the cord is cut. We call that the miracle of birth. I don't know what the baby calls it— perhaps it's good that we can't recall.

While here, I am undergoing a transformation. Being here did not cause the transformation; that began some time ago. This experience only magnifies the intensity of the change.

I don't think that my experience is any different from others'. Oh, I realize that everyone doesn't experience the isolation of prison. Yet, I believe that we all have our times of intense trials and struggles. Times when, through illness or loss, separation or death, we find ourselves alone and hanging on by that last strand.

I don't think, no matter how nicely we paint the picture, that we can honestly say we like that desperate feeling. However, every positive change—every jump to a higher level of energy and awareness—requires us to go through a period of discomfort, just like birth.

I believe that all of us have the choice of when lessons come to us. At least, at the spiritual level, we have that choice. Intuitively, we will know when the time is right. Likewise, it is within our power to be the victim or the victor. When, however, we permit others to make our decisions or responses for us; when we do what others say should be done; when we act as others say we should act; when we allow someone, some group or something to direct our lives; we learn practically nothing. These actions may reduce conflict. However, a life free of conflict produces no growth.

I may have experienced physical prison, but many people live in prisons created by their own choosing. It is impossible to change our circumstances without experiencing the full knowledge of how we got there. Prison, for me, allowed the time to look at myself and the choices that resulted in my physical confinement.

> I may have experienced physical prison, but many people
> live in prisons created by their own choosing.

A few hours after I wrote the above journal entry, I was able to observe a real life example of choices that had negative consequences. Two men in my prison unit began teasing each other, engaging in horseplay that quickly degenerated. For the first time since my arrival, I witnessed a full-fledged fight—cuts, blood, and all.

Here were two men who both knew that fighting in a minimum security facility carried dramatic consequences. Not only did the two physically hurt each other, but they also suffered the immediate consequences of detention and transfer. Both were shipped to a federal prison with bars, fences, razor wire, and inmates who have little regard for others.

We could feel sorry for these two inmates, or we could understand the truth that we get exactly what we need to grow and learn. They will either move through life lessons without peace, or come to understand the larger spiritual picture. This is not unlike the challenges that everyone faces every day.

Peace is obtained when we are aware of the larger spiritual picture. Unfortunately, most people have only a limited awareness, if any, of their roles in co-creation. By being consciously aware of our role as co-creators in our earthly plight, we come to an awareness of the "big picture." Hence, when someone treats us unkindly, when harmless circumstances erode into an altercation, or when things just don't seem to be going our way, we can stop and understand that what is happening is for our higher learning. At that point, the momentary impact of the event becomes clearer and more meaningful.

As we grow and learn, as we work on our mission, we have the opportunity to serve humanity in some way. Every positive change involves a period of discomfort. These men were clearly in a state of discomfort, the effect of which may last for years. In prison, I experienced a state of discomfort limited by time. Yet I know that I created this experience by my choices. However, I felt safe in my circumstances and peaceful regardless of what was happening around me.

For much of my life, my understanding of the lessons involved was veiled. I just couldn't see the "big picture." Answers are given through our higher selves as we need them and as we are ready for them—and not before. Why not have the answers placed before us, since we are spirit? Why go through the process of learning when God can just give us the answers?

Let's look at it from another perspective that might illustrate that truth. If an individual went to a university's medical school to learn neurosurgery, and the instructor gave the class the answers to the tests so they would pass, would the students have learned anything significant about neurosurgery? More importantly, would you want them to perform brain surgery on your mother?

Learning is no different for us. It is important to understand how we learn. Having the answers before the question arises or before we understand we need them is tantamount to having a plethora of useless facts. Answers are useful only when they come in the context of learning or growth experiences.

In prison, I felt as if I were in an abyss. Sometimes we have to go through hell to get to heaven. Don't discount that statement. For many, that is true. Lessons learned, spiritual journeys taken, are often fraught with serious obstacles and tests. Through the test of fire, we often come to learn the strength of character. While the fire burns, that is also where the metal is tested and hardened.

"We're in what some would call a dog kennel."

Bruce, my work partner and fellow inmate, began speaking as we returned from lunch.

"Think of it. It's Wednesday, so we're sitting here in the top of a metal building, sweltering heat, no ventilation, and sweat popping up on our foreheads. All around us is a tall, grey, metal cage with only one way in and the same way out. Day in and day out, we have to be here. This is the base location of our work assignment."

His description was accurate. The place wasn't so bad now, but in midsummer it became a hellhole, an environment not fit for any human.

Bruce then continued with a profound statement. "You know, I feel freer here than at the prison compound."

There was a gentleness in his eyes as he spoke those words, and I understood. As prisoners, it's hard to find comforting feelings like freedom and happiness. When we do, we treat those experiences as precious gems. They are hard to come by, especially in a system that is designed to punish—one that tries to remove human dignity from life, which probably serves mostly to continue the decay of the prisoner. I wonder if this system rehabilitates or perpetuates crime? Somehow, I know that rehabilitation happens only by the strength of the person who makes that choice. It does not come from some institution saying it is so.

Many days passed in prison with introspective thoughts occupying my mind. Some would call prison hell, yet I came to understand some measure of peace and happiness there. Truth is, the stronger and more spiritually aware we are, the happier we can become. Happiness is obtained by giving, not by seeking to get. Therefore, the more we learn and grow, the more we can serve as a positive influence in the world. Influence is not limited to being in a certain place or doing a certain thing. We can influence where we are in our daily lives. With that understanding, we can be happy anywhere.

In *No Ordinary Moments*, Dan Millman illustrates some of this truth: "Once, I was driving on a curving road. A car going in the opposite direction passed me, and the driver yelled out her window at mo, 'Pig!' I felt very upset at being called a pig by a complete stranger. 'She probably has a problem with men,' I thought, as I rounded the curve—and nearly ran over a pig in the middle of the road." What he said, in a unique way, illustrates the fact that much of life is a matter of perspective.

We can't always understand what's happening around us, why we are where we are, and what's around the next corner. What we interpret as bad can be a rich blessing in disguise. Those blessings, in unusual ways, even come while in prison.

Friday – February 23, 1996 – Journal

Today has been a beautiful day outside. I'm beginning to find simple blessings in things like sunny days, squirrels at play, and birds in flight. I know it sounds simpleminded, but I wonder how often we take for granted the blessings that surround us? If nothing else thus far, prison has taught me to become more observant and appreciative of what we do have.

Yesterday, for example, I was touched by a song that the choir sang. It's easy for me to connect with the

music, but I sometimes miss the beauty and meaning
of the words. The song we sang touched me on both
counts—music and words. I thought of the painful lessons
we all must, at one time or another, face. I wanted to
share the words of this song, written by Babbie Mason,
in hopes that they may touch a chord in your heart.

> All things work for our good
> though sometimes we can't see how they could.
> Struggles that break our hearts in two
> sometimes blind us to the truth.
> Our Father knows what's best for us;
> His ways are not our own.
> So, when your pathway grows dim,
> and you just can't see Him,
> Remember He's still on the throne.
> God is too wise to be mistaken.
> God is too good to be unkind.
> So when you don't understand,
> when you don't see His plan,
> When you can't trace His hand, trust His heart.
> He sees the Master plan.
> He holds the future in His hands.
> So don't live as those who have no hope.
> All our hope is found in Him.
> We walk in present knowledge,
> but He sees the first and the last.
> And like a tapestry, He's weaving you and me
> to someday be just like Him.
> God is too wise to be mistaken.
> God is too good to be unkind.
> So when you don't understand,

when you don't see His plan,

When you can't trace His hand, trust His heart.

He alone is faithful and true

He alone knows what's best for you...

God is too wise to be mistaken.

God is too good to be unkind.

There is great beauty in this song, for no matter what our station is in life, our spiritual path moves us forward to ultimately reunite with the Creator. While I may not like the pain and toil, I do know that it's for my higher good. That knowledge provides me peace of mind and an inner calm that helps me get through each day. I may not see His plan now, but I have the assurance that it is at work in my life and that through this experience —prison—I am learning many lessons.

So when you don't understand,

when you don't see His plan,

When you can't trace His hand, trust His heart.

Traveling backward, reaching dark places in my mind, and remembering what got me in prison is painful at times. I would guess this is true for all of us. To understand where we are going, we have to know clearly where we have been. Knowing where we have been and truly understanding the lessons empower us to choose a pathway to more positive consequences. Every consequence is based, in large part, on our awareness of what choices we make and why.

I experienced physical prison. Most who read this have not. For all of us, though, we have experienced prison at one time in our lives. It could be the prison of self-hate or the prison of poverty or shame. Our prisons may be the addiction to food as an emotional comfort, or estrangement from our loved ones over cross words in years past.

Whatever prison we find ourselves in, there are truly lessons to be learned that are the keys to unlocking the doors into the future. They are the keys to making different choices, thereby releasing the chains that bind us and freeing us from our prisons.

14

From Adversity to Purpose

Stepping back through the front doors I had entered five months earlier, I walked twenty-three steps to the van where seven other inmates and four prison guards prepared to leave. We were not being released! Rather, we were on a mission of goodwill. Our group, called "Community Outreach," was planning to speak to students at a local middle school. Our message was, "Don't do what we did. Look where it got us!"

Often people ask me if I have found my life's purpose. Some find it in school; others find it through their jobs. I found mine through the most unusual of experiences—prison.

February 29 is a day I will never forget. Of course, it would be my luck to be put in prison on a leap year. This was the first day out of the prison compound and off the Air Force Base.

Federal prison camp Seymour Johnson is located on the grounds of the Seymour Johnson Air Force Base in Goldsboro, North Carolina. It's referred to by some as "Club Fed" for the perceived presence of swimming pools, tennis courts, or movie stars. To be honest, I resent that perception. It is far from the truth. The prison facilities are physically decent, albeit with no tennis courts or swimming pools; however, they were run by people who love to exercise their power over people who are already powerless. Prison is punishment, and the employees here want to make that so. No place and no part of prison is a cake-walk. To be sure, it is "Fed," but there is no "Club" about it!

Stepping back through the front doors felt good. Somehow, I was selected to participate in this program, and I could not have been more excited. For once, I felt that somehow I had some value, something to offer.

As we prepared to leave, there was an air of positive energy around us. We were now getting ready to share ourselves through our stories. Perhaps we eventually learn that the quality of each moment depends not on what we get from it, but on what we bring to it. These were quality moments. We approached this opportunity with a spirit of excitement, enthusiasm, and expectancy.

Each of us, in our green uniforms and polished work boots, boarded the van. We were reminded by staff that our behavior was important. After all, we were inmates, and the prison made sure we never forgot that. "Keep in mind, many people in society don't want to see you out. They think that you have nothing to offer. Rather, you're lowlife criminals. Don't give them any reason to support their opinions." With that last admonition, we rolled out.

I couldn't have been happier during that moment and the moments that followed. You can find happiness anytime, even in prison. It's up to us to find the good in any moment. What is the alternative—despair? We must understand what would lead us to feel despair or depressed, and once that understanding comes, then we can choose to feel happy rather than depressed. I certainly did not want the depression. I had enough of that.

Happiness is a state of being, not something that just happens, but something we choose. It is what we bring to life, accessible anytime—moment to moment. For me, happiness came from love. On that day I was getting ready to share with others in love, telling them what had happened to me and how choices create consequences. Somehow the sharing of the experience and the journey helped ease some of the pain in me. It was also a way to give back to society, and that is happiness.

As we drove through the Air Force Base gates, for the first time in five months, I saw the freedom that I had left behind. My heart ached at what I had left behind, yet rejoiced to be able to experience being out that day. To someone who has never lost freedom, it is hard to understand. I know I created the circumstances to lose my freedom, but the experience of freedom that day had the same value. Perhaps because I did choose this course in my life, I felt in awe as I found myself looking at the traffic lights, cars traveling on the highways, roadside signs, and so many other things that we daily take for granted. They hit me in a profound way: that the ability to drive to work, to choose your job, to select the route you want to take, and to eat what you want for breakfast are all freedoms that we ignore. I never gave them much thought. Being denied freedom, however, magnifies the intensity and appreciation of what we do have, even the little things. This day, my first true day away from prison, reminded me of the value of what, by my actions, I was forced to leave behind.

> Being denied freedom, however, magnifies the intensity and appreciation of what we do have, even the little things.

Crisis offers opportunities to reach the deepest level of our being. Through this experience, I came to know myself in ways previously unknown, and through that I gained new understandings. After five months and much spiritual introspection, I fully understood. It felt as if it was a fully integrated part of my being. After all, I actively worked to create the situation for my learning. Further, I knew that what I was getting ready to do was closely attached to my mission in life. Coming to prison was no accident. Something worthwhile was in process.

After a brief ride, we arrived at the school where we were to speak. As we unloaded from the van, I really had no idea what to expect.

Others who had gone out before told me of their experiences, but that still doesn't take the place of my own experience. I wasn't feeling apprehensive; rather, I was feeling a little excited.

I wondered how we would be received. At the prison, staff members often looked right through us as if we didn't exist. *Would that be the case at the school?* I wondered to myself. Being "looked through" is a disconcerting feeling. Frankly, I was hoping that our treatment might be better in the real world. I missed being seen as a person.

Rain was threatening, and it was overcast and dreary as we walked into the school. The middle school housed children from the fifth to the eighth grade. I suppose when I was a small child, I was in awe of adults, especially adult visitors to my school. Therefore, you can imagine what these children thought when eight adult men in prison uniforms came walking in. I would like to have had a camera to catch the expressions on some of their faces. I knew some were unsure and some were scared, but all I could think of was to smile and ask my spiritual self to let them know they had nothing to fear. If communication comes from the heart in love, it will be received and contribute to others' growth, whether they recognize it or not. This was my second opportunity to share my story with others, and I certainly wanted to share in love.

The principal met with the staff member in charge, and we were divided into groups and given our mission. This principal wanted to make a difference in the lives of her students. Only months before, a number of the students had been caught with drugs and weapons on campus, and the principal wanted to stem the tide of bad behavior. Older kids were hustling younger ones, and for a middle school, the crime rate was bad. Of course, the children assumed that because of their ages, they could get by with most anything and not be punished.

We come to maturity as human beings when we take conscious responsibility for our own actions. This responsibility comes the moment we realize that the world we see is a reflection of our mental state. Our conflicts, problems, and dissatisfactions originate from a dependence on the outside world to satisfy us, to make us happy. When that doesn't happen, we need to look within ourselves to determine what it is we are seeking from the external world.

Often, today, I hear from people who, like me, are facing significant consequences from the choices they made. They ask for help, but rarely want to accept responsibility for their actions or see the connection of their choices to the consequences they are facing. The same is true now as was true then; every choice has a consequence. Our role that day was to help the youngsters understand that simple concept.

We couldn't expect children to understand all that was presented. Some concepts of crime would not make sense to them. Yet, while they might not understand it all, we could explain the concept and make an impression. In fact, children are often more receptive to spiritual truth than adults. Our objective was to get through to the children and help them see that they are responsible and can make good decisions, good choices.

A fellow prisoner, Ted, and I teamed together. Our first stop was a sixth-grade class. Simple mathematics told me that the children were mostly twelve years old. As we approached the room with our staff escort, the teacher emerged, greeted the three of us, and welcomed us into her class. Apparently, they were anticipating us.

"Class, this is Mr. Baker. He's from the Federal Prison Camp at Seymour Johnson and brought with him two gentlemen who want to speak to you."

I can't tell you how my heart beamed as I heard this kind lady refer to us as "gentlemen." That was a term that I had not heard in many months and a concept of self that had almost disappeared. Months of being ignored and degraded had taken their toll on my self-esteem. The full impact didn't hit me until that moment when she used the word "gentlemen." I wondered if that was my problem or part of the purpose of prison. My guess was that it was a little of both. I would later wonder if the prison's intent to degrade and control human beings actually contributed to the re-offending rate of some. Many never seem to feel they have value again.

Mr. Baker explained to the class our purpose for being there as little eyes scanned Ted and me. Some of them had never seen prisoners before, and they weren't sure what to expect. How could they? Many had lived a very protected life. I was filled with awe as I realized the importance of our visit there that day. If sharing our experience would keep one person from choosing the wrong path, then reparations to the community would have been successful.

Ted was a big man, so as he stood to speak he commanded the students' attention. "I see some of you students have DARE on your shirts. What does that stand for?"

The students responded that it meant to stay off of drugs.

"Right," Ted responded. "Well, in my day, 'dare' meant to do something wrong that someone encouraged or pushed you to do. I started my life of crime on a dare. Peer pressure got me, and now I'm a federal prisoner."

Ted began his speech, and it was a marvelous presentation. He explained how at age thirteen he started drinking and getting into trouble because of peer pressure. From there, he progressed to smoking marijuana to fit in with the "in" crowd. "Just fitting in, you know, just fitting in."

I could tell by the looks on the faces of the children in the class that they were captured by his story. He told of his children and how he had straightened his life out. For years, he lived a normal, productive life. Then one day, his daughter called, needing money—money that Ted didn't have. So he went to his brother to borrow the funds. His brother gave him the funds, no repayment necessary, and an ounce of cocaine. His brother said, "You can have as much money as you need as long as you just sell the drugs."

Ted responded in fear, knowing that he knew nothing about selling drugs, especially cocaine. "Oh, don't worry, bro. I'll get one of my boys to do it for you."

After that first innocent weekend with his brother, Ted returned home with fourteen thousand dollars in his pocket and drugs to sell in his hand.

From the higher perspective of spiritual knowledge, we can look back and know that things we now interpret as negative offer the greatest opportunity for growth and new beginnings. This was true for Ted. He stood before these students sharing the darkest parts of his former self as he embarked on his new beginning, one started in prison.

From the higher perspective of spiritual knowledge,
we can look back and know that things we now interpret as negative
offer the greatest opportunity for growth and new beginnings.

One of the most important lessons we can learn as humans is that when we fail, the sky doesn't fall. Oh, the outcome may not be judged to be good, that's for sure. But we're here to learn and give help to others while they learn. Therein, we find meaning to the outcome.

Ted continued. "I took the wrong path. I wanted to be the 'Mac Daddy' of my town. With a .357 strapped to my side, I was looked up to as the supplier."

As Ted spoke those words, I respected him. He did not glamorize what he did. Of course, he had the trappings of the outward success that drug money brings, but now he was past that. It is not unlike my experience. Yes, they were different issues, but the journey was the same: wanting the outward appearances of success.

"Kids, the only things you get out of drugs are 'P.P.D.' Remember that. Prison, Poverty, or Death! My brother, who turned me on to selling drugs, told me: 'Never be a user of your product.' Well, when I was at the penitentiary in Atlanta, I got a call. You see, my brother didn't follow his own advice. He became a user of his product. The temptation was just too great. The person on the other end of the line told me my brother died. His heart just burst while doing crack cocaine."

As Ted spoke those words, I knew that deep in his heart, he hurt. Ted drew the prison and poverty card for his drug experience. His brother drew death!

The children seemed spellbound as they heard Ted's deep, resounding voice. He was there to do a job. He told them how he used young people, just like them, to do his drug delivery work. If they got in trouble, another drug dealer hurt them. They were expendable, used as pawns in a deadly game.

He admonished them to be aware and stay away from drugs. He didn't paint a pretty picture. Then again, it wasn't pretty for him, either. While in prison, he saw grown men get raped and others get knifed to death. All the while, he had no choice but to just walk on by. Self-preservation defines the rules. For his drug activity, he received a 123-month sentence. Ten years and three months was almost as long as some of those children had been alive. Ted wished someone had told him the truth as he told them.

At one time, I would have never been able to understand a story like Ted's. I would have judged him harshly. Yet, I was right there with him getting ready to share my story. Both of us were working to find meaning out of adversity.

Sometimes our suffering enables us to understand others. Along with the pain of suffering comes the blessing of compassion. There is a gift that can be found in adversity. It doesn't make the adversity any easier; it only makes it more meaningful. There was much beauty and meaning in what Ted had to share.

When we are troubled with a sense of unworthiness, such feelings manifest themselves through illness, accidents, failures, or other forms of self-sabotage. How well I understood this. A lot of soul-searching led me to the understanding that I had set up my own failures principally out of an overall feeling of unworthiness and abandonment. The desire for all the outward trappings that led me to the choice of theft was only a way to try and compensate for those feelings. Because it wasn't who I was, it would never satisfy and ultimately lead to my downfall. It only confirmed those beliefs I had about myself. Yet, it saved my life and put me back in touch with my soul.

My turn to speak and share my story of failure was soon to come. Sharing openly and honestly does not come easy. In fact, it forces us to visit the dark places—those places we have built tall walls around to shelter us from the pain. Intuitively, I knew this was good.

In order to be filled with light and move forward in spirit, we learn self-worth. Wo, in fact, may get the message that lourning those feelings are why we are here, at least in part. Whether we're clearing old karmas or have other reasons for feeling as we do, self-worth rises when we learn that our overall benefit for existence as humans is learning, growth, and giving in love. As we apply ourselves in helping others, we also help ourselves. That is what makes the pitfalls in our journeys become diamonds in our life.

As we apply ourselves in helping others, we also help ourselves. That is what makes the pitfalls in our journeys become diamonds in our life.

I was there because I cared. I felt somehow that sharing my experience with these children might have an impact. Like dropping a pebble in a still pond, the ripples can be far-reaching. My motives were not self-serving, as often in the past. Self-serving feelings do not demonstrate an attitude of true service. Humility, gratitude, and an overall knowledge that we're in this together—these define true service, which is the essence of love.

"Stay in school. You can be somebody!" With those last comments, Ted finished. With a deliberateness in his step, he left the front of the classroom. There was silence. It was now my turn to speak.

There is no greater joy to me than speaking before groups of people. In my not-too-distant past, I traveled the country speaking to and teaching as many as six hundred people. Never before, however, had I been in this role as a speaker.

I can't speak for others, but often I find some of the best material for my speaking only moments before it's my turn to speak. Such was the case that day.

"You can be somebody!" That comment rushed over me like a wave crashing against the seashore in Maine. That was the link; that was the connection that resonated throughout me.

As Ted was concluding, I silently bowed in prayer. *Dear God, open my heart and use my mouth to speak a message that is in line with your will. Allow my spiritual self to connect in love with the spiritual selves of these children. May they receive good from what is said. Thank you for using me as your spiritual instrument. Amen.*

My prayer, Ted's conclusion, and my new opening seemed to happen simultaneously. I walked to the front of the classroom and, with a peaceful love in my heart, looked at the bright-eyed youngsters and began to speak. "My name is Gallagher, 11642-058. That number is how I am known. You see, I am a convicted felon serving time in a federal prison." Those were the first words spoken to this group of students and the beginning of my story, a journey begun long ago.

When we come to love, to understand, and to accept ourselves, that love and acceptance will generate in us the heroic efforts and commitment to stop our self-destructive behaviors and become masters of our destiny. Sharing with these students was one way that Ted and I could do something positive for others as well as for ourselves.

"Let me ask you a question. How do you know if a person is 'somebody'? How would you know that someone coming into your school is important?"

We are told not to judge. That seems easier said than done. Based on what I had received thus far, I was not sure how I would judge the situation and the people involved. At that time, I had some limited understanding that something larger was taking place. All I knew was that I should feel tolerance and patience.

As architects of our own lessons, we always have the answers to our lessons within ourselves. We can access the answers any time we choose, through spiritual awareness and communication with our souls. Choice, however, involves more than saying, "I'm ready." Real choice means that we go deeper. We try to find the true meaning of the experience and what we are meant to learn. This was true as I sought to apply my efforts as an inmate speaking to the children.

The children were anxious to respond to my questions.

"If you dressed nice," one child responded.

Another said, "It's where you live."

A young lady to my right, in an exasperated voice, said, "That's not what makes you somebody. It's how you feel in your heart," My, how her light seemed to shine! The beam on her face warmed my heart.

Many of the children equated the "importance of being somebody" with exterior appearances. I understood. I felt the same thing only years earlier, which led to the choices that landed me in prison. Had I understood years ago that being somebody was in my heart and soul, perhaps my path would have gone another way. Then again, perhaps the lessons I am learning today would have only been postponed for another time.

At birth, we all have limitations. This is not meant to imply that we are inferior, but rather, because of our humanness, we need limitations so that the tests and lessons we encounter will allow for our growth. The limitation in my case was, in part, a feeling of wanting to be somebody.

"Kids, if I drove to the front of your school in a BMW 850i, would I be somebody?"

Some of the children shook their heads yes as others said, "sure."

"What if I got out of the car, came into your school in a tailored double-breasted suit with a gold Rolex watch on—would I be somebody?"

"You'd be the man," one little boy said excitedly.

"Yeah, he'd be the man," another spoke out.

"Well, kids, I used to think the same thing. But today I stand here before you as a prisoner. Definitely not 'the man!'

"Two months ago, while I was having lunch in the prison chow hall, a guy looked over at me, and in a very judgmental way asked me, 'Hey man, have you ever been in the projects?' I thought it funny that he asked me this question. I could tell in his voice that he thought that I knew nothing of poverty and shame. He judged me harshly. I could feel the bitterness in his words. My response shocked him.

"'Yeah, I've lived in the projects. What about you?' He didn't answer. He was too taken aback by my response. How could a clean-cut white guy know anything about the streets? He judged me by my looks as often we judge others. However, what is inside cannot often be seen from the surface."

My time was limited, however. I shared with the children my past upbringing. I wanted them to know that I understood living in functional poverty. Now that I look back, I didn't think of myself as poor. Never in my life have my needs not been met. "When I was two years old, my father died. That left me in my mother's sole care. Her work skills were limited, so often she worked in a textile mill or did janitorial work. She did whatever she could to take care of our needs. I remember her telling me, 'Son, you can be somebody.'"

I was determined to live up to that expectation. Little did I know that I had been implanted with seeds of believing that I was unworthy and really a nobody. Through speaking those words, I wanted the children to know that I could identify with them all: rich or poor, black or white. My upbringing was monetarily poor, but rich and varied with many experiences.

As I spoke to the children, I felt a sort of calm and compassion wash over me. Somehow, and in some way, the Spirit was at work for my benefit as well as their benefit. It was not me speaking, but rather, the Spirit was working through me. Failures can become stepping stones between us and our true goals. I was sharing my failures in hopes that the lesson might help others as they journey through their lessons. In my case, failures often occurred many times before I finally found success. As I continued to fail, my spirit was learning, growing and finding success. Perhaps that was the true meaning of success.

"When I came up through school, I wasn't in the 'in crowd.' Some might have considered me a nerd. I just knew that the only way to be 'somebody' was to stay in school, do what the teachers said, and get an education."

All that I said to the students there was positive, bringing a good message. Unfortunately, I was an example of failure after doing all the right things.

"After high school, I went to the university, completed my education, and got a good job. I worked as a CPA. That's a person who helps people by managing their money and calculating their taxes."

I wanted the children to know that success can come through doing the right things. Next, however, I was going to share the dark side of my activities, the time of life when I made "bad" choices.

Choice and change involve giving up something we want for something we want more. After seemingly achieving success in school, college, and work, I was ready to make additional choices. These choices, unlike others already made, were going to have a profound impact on my life. These choices would be a radical departure from the choices I made earlier in life. These choices would change my life forever.

Consider the rules: (1) we only get one body, (2) we all learn lessons, (3) lessons often appear as mistakes or failures, (4) a lesson is repeated until learned, (5) if we don't learn the lessons the first time, they are repeated and get harder, (6) we know we've learned the lessons when our actions change, (7) we tend to forget the rules when we've learned the lessons, and (8) we can remember the rules any time we wish. I recall seeing "the rules" in outline form somewhere and, at the time, they made perfect sense. They still do. More times than not, when I talk with people who face prisons of their own and find from their choices that they have been released, they will agree that the above eight items are truth in simple form.

What's the point? We are much more than we seem. We know that we are here to learn and to evolve spiritually. Learning the lessons is our choice, not a requirement. We choose whether to open the door of opportunity and learn or to leave it closed and wait for another chance. My mistakes and failures have provided for me the greatest opportunity for growth—especially spiritual growth—that I have received to date. I have learned practical principles that, when applied to daily life, are profound. But more, much more benefit has been gained from a broader universal understanding that has come from the lessons.

Sometimes it may sound as if I am excited about failure. I'm not. However, I've come to learn that those who ride the waves of change through learning and growth will soar into the future; those who resist will learn that resistance creates pain. I have felt pain in failure and continue to do so. However, over time I have learned that focusing on the bigger picture helps me put painful experiences into perspective.

Saturday – March 30, 1996 – Journal

8:58 a.m. Thank goodness today is a new day. Suffering happens. Fortunately, it doesn't last forever. For that, I am thankful. Yesterday, for whatever reason, I felt deeply the pain and loss and separation. It's said that every pain endured contains a lesson to be learned. Well, yesterday the lesson must have been big.

Last night, as I laid my head on my pillow to go to sleep, I cried. It had been a while since I allowed myself to go deep inside and feel. But last night, I went to that dark place. I see daily the pictures of my two children and I can't come close to describing the immense loss I feel due to our separation. Rob, my eldest son, wrote me a note which said, "I miss you so bad, I see you in my dreams." Talk about tearing your heart out! That will do it. Then, on occasion—more than once, in fact—Alex asked, "Just why did you do it anyway, Dad?" I long to be able to give him a good, logical answer. How do you tell a child that the struggles we face in life are for our growth and that good can be found in adversity? I don't know exactly how to explain that truth. The only thing I do know is that there is no amount of money that could replace what I've missed and lost in not being with my children.

Alabama (the musical group) has a song out entitled "In Pictures." The song tells of a father's pain in seeing his children grow up through pictures. I can identify with that song. Thanksgiving, Rob's birthday, Christmas, New Year's, the '96 snowstorms, Valentine's Day, and now Alex's birthday were all, for me, visits only in pictures. Every time I hear that song, I am emotionally whipped around like a marionette.

Thankfully, in the absence of my children and a loving relationship, I have been blessed by many supportive friends. Through their support and God's spiritual guidance, for the most part I am successful in shifting my perspective so I can appreciate and value whatever happens. Obviously, that doesn't mean pain, hurt, and other emotions aren't felt due to loss. They are, and I grieve their losses. Yet our biggest challenges and opportunities for growth often involve separations, death, accidents, illness, pain, or other forms of personal loss.

When we come to the point that we actively accept whatever is happening as part of our process of learning and growth, we can more easily accept what is taking place. There are no mistakes. Eventually, if we are willing to grow, we develop the faith to know that there is an inherent wisdom and meaning in what is taking place. Trust me. That trust, faith or wisdom does not eliminate the pain. No. The pain still hurts. Our faith, however, does allow us to accept with serenity where we are.

I am here, and you are where you are, to learn from each person, each situation, and every challenge we face. On a spiritual level, we are loved deeply. Yes, we as humans feel pain, but we each have a special role to play. As we immerse ourselves, being fully present in the moment, and become aware of what is happening, we open the doors to greater understandings and growth.

Birth involves labor pains, even though we are the ones being born. This whole process is much like rebirth. The pain is different, but in many ways the process is the same.

When the day passed and all inmates were accounted for, we left the school where we had spent the better part of a day. My heart was singing with joy, and those feelings were, in my opinion, shared by all. For one brief moment, we had put aside our self-centered feelings and focused on what we could give to others. On that day, I felt a shift. Not only did we do something worthwhile for the students who were present, but also we became people rather than just numbers to those who supported this effort in the prison system. Sure, I was still 11642-058, but after that meeting and others that followed, the prison guards referred to me by my name, not my number.

As we made our way back to the prison compound, I found solace in silence. I knew that I had experienced a defining moment and that a shift had taken place. What the future would hold, I didn't know. I suppose that I was still in a lesson at that point—the lesson of embracing the moment and being present. While the future seemed grey and undefined, I knew that sharing my experience in hopes that others would benefit would become a significant part of my future.

Prison, whatever kind of prison you might find yourself in, is a place that is dark, a place where success and optimism are rarely found. That is true whether your prison is real or self-imposed from some hidden choice you've made. Regardless of form, finding purpose, meaning, or success in prison is difficult at best. Yet, some of the most profound leaders of our time have come from the depths of prison and risen like phoenixes out of the ashes to provide hope and inspiration to others.

Look at your place today. Ask yourself: what is keeping me from achieving the greatness I am here to do? What is holding me back? Whatever the answer or answers, those are your prisons. In order to escape those chains that bind us, we must be willing to look into our prison experience, find out what choices were made that got us where we are, and identify what choices we can make to set ourselves free and claim our life's purpose. No one said it is easy. It was not for me. In fact, speaking and writing about the experience is a blessing. It keeps me grounded in the awareness that I have to be vigilant about remembering that every choice has a consequence. The choices we make daily are the choices that can open the door to positive results and freedom.

15

Lights Out—Tomorrow Will Be Different

———— ◆ ————

Some people say they hear a voice when God speaks. Others say they just have a knowing. Still others struggle to know their direction in life and where they fit in the big scheme of things or, as some would call it, God's plan. I was blessed. As soon as I left the prison compound to speak to the young people, and especially after I saw their faces when we spoke to them, I knew beyond a shadow of a doubt that the pain of the consequences I was experiencing was all for good.

I don't mean to imply that life in prison became easier after that first experience; it didn't. Consequences are consequences, and I've come to believe that we must go through whatever experience we need in order to achieve our ultimate objective, our life purpose. It isn't a destination. It is a journey fraught with many experiences, all of which are designed to give us what we need ultimately to succeed in this lifetime.

As we crawled back into the prison van for our trip back to what was then home, I felt that something had happened that would be life-changing, for the better. After the first experience, we were allowed three other off-premises speaking engagements during my incarceration. Each one gave me continued assurance that the path and the direction I felt was right.

One thing that resonated within me was the critical importance of being aware of the choices I made and the impact those choices would have in the future. If every choice has a consequence, then it was important to not only look to the future of my release, but also, to make good choices in whatever situation I found myself in as those choices would become the foundation of my life moving forward.

For the next five months, I felt an anxious anticipation about what would happen when I received the word that I would be free or that I would face limited freedom. As an inmate, I could either serve my entire sentence or seek to finish my incarceration in a halfway house. The opportunity to have increased freedom, to work, and to be back in the "real world" was the only choice for me, although there was no guarantee that I would be given that privilege. My choices and behavior while in prison would have a direct impact on the speed of my release.

Most human beings generally live in the past, present, or future. As a future person, I was challenged by my inability to control my future destiny. The past I could not change. That was easy for me to accept. The present seemed boring to me. The future was always, to me, where the excitement was. However, in prison I had no control over the future. I was a number. My life, in many ways, was not my own. The only control I had in prison was choosing how to live out the experience.

Those wiser than I have said that the experiences we find ourselves in are exactly what we need for our best growth. I can imagine that many who read these words would disagree with that statement. It is difficult to accept that if we find ourselves in a situation that we don't like, such as prison, a severe illness, or losing a child, that experience could be for my highest and best good. During my prison experience, I would not have agreed, either. Now I see that everything that happened was necessary to give me the experience and personal growth needed to accomplish what I came to this life to accomplish.

A dear friend of mine, several years back, found that her husband was diagnosed with terminal cancer. Their life was turned upside-down and shattered with the news that their time together would be limited and focused on medical procedures. There is no doubt in my mind that she would have rather had most anything than what she was facing. Like most people, she had the same feelings, doubts, angers, and the other range of emotions that anyone in her situation would face. At that time, his illness became her prison.

Her husband has since made his transition, and she has courageously moved forward with her life. The point is, however, she has also taken this experience as a caregiver and found value in helping others. Betty Garrett's book, *From Hiccups to Hospice*, is a shining example of how one can take the darkness of a prison experience and turn it into value for others. At this point, a large part of her life purpose is to make a difference in the lives of others.

From those first twenty-three steps into prison, for a good six months I tried to hang on to my past life and control outcomes. My identity was defined by what I did, by my career, by my titles as Sales Manager and Daddy. However, in prison that identity was stripped from me, and I was only a number. With identity stripped and ego severely bruised, I struggled to find out who I was. As the days of spring lengthened into the light of summer, I found myself less concerned with who I was and more focused on what small joys I could capture from each day. When you take the time to be still, so still that the squirrels will approach and eat from your hand, you tend to become very present. You know that whatever happens, it will all work out in the end.

Sometime in the middle of summer, I received a call to come to one of the prison official's offices. When called, you go, as it is not something you choose to ignore. My anticipation was high as I had requested release to a halfway house. Living in a halfway house is still prison, mind you, but it is certainly a freer environment.

"I'm sorry, Gallagher. It doesn't look like your request will be approved." As I heard those words, my hopes were dashed, and my heart sank. I had counted on this form of release, thinking that I had learned what I needed to know. Surely they should have seen it my way. Others were released and soon returned. I knew that I would use this limited freedom wisely. Why they couldn't see that was beyond me.

"Why?" I asked as politely as possible, working hard to keep a stiff upper lip.

"Looks like our count might be down, so the warden is holding off on any halfway house approvals," the case manager said in a matter-of-fact voice.

What became clear in that instant was that prison was a business. Yes, there may very well be a spiritual component to the experience on a higher level, but make no mistake, inmates are a commodity that is needed to make sure the machine works. If there is a shortage, either too many being released or not enough coming in, that affects the census, or count. The count needs to be maintained at a sustainable level for the prison.

As I made my way back to my cell, I felt like a pawn in play. I felt disappointed and angry. "More time stuck here," I grumbled to myself, as I could feel the expectation of a summer release dashing before my eyes. Buck could sense that there was something wrong as I entered our cell.

"What's up, Chuck?" he asked with an upbeat cheer in his voice. He knew something was wrong. We had become close, and intuitively he knew that I had received some disturbing news.

"They're not approving my halfway house, Buck."

"I was afraid of that," he responded. "Let me guess, the count?"

"How did you know?" I was amazed by his response. I mean, where did he get his information?

"Happens every summer," Buck said. "For some reason it seems that they get worried every summer about the count and start delaying or denying releases. They'll probably grant it; just give them time."

Buck was generally not the prophet of hope, so I was surprised—not only with his knowledge of the situation, but also with his insight to hope. Then he followed all this up with one last statement. "Chuck, all you can do is one day at a time!" And with those words, he walked out. He spoke the exact words I needed to hear. If there are angels among us, I can't help but believe that, for me, Buck was an angel.

Some of my dearest friends today are open about their abuse of alcohol. They have said that they take one day at a time. One day of sobriety moves to the next and now some thirty years later, one commented that he'd been sober thirty years. Then, just as quickly, he shared that it is still one day at a time for him. I suppose in retrospect, that is true for me as well. In fact, it is my guess that one day at a time is true for most people. I am still reminded daily of the impact of choices and have to remain aware that every choice, even the seemingly insignificant ones, has a consequence.

As I finished dinner that late June evening, I went out on the compound for a quiet walk alone. The closest thing to a walking trail or track we had was a one-third mile gravel loop around the recreation yard. I can't begin to count how many times I walked that circle, thinking most of the time and quieting my mind the rest. So often, people talk of meditation. Well, I found the repetition of an oval walk calming and clearing.

On about the tenth loop, I began to understand that once again, I was trying to control the outcome—just like my past behavior. And, once again, I was reminded that I was not in control. I could make choices that could affect the outcome, but I couldn't control it because it was not mine to control. It never was. I could control my choices in the present, but the past is the past and the future was not in my control.

Even in the worst environment I could imagine—prison—I was still clothed, fed and had my needs met. No different than the lilies of the field. If they could be cared for, so could I. The biggest challenge was accepting that all was happening according to plan. It was quite a revelation finally to understand that I didn't control the plan. Yet, most every time I might begin to believe that I did, I would find that something happened unexpectedly to make me understand—I didn't. The denial of my request this afternoon was just another reminder.

Weeks passed as I continued to hone my weed-eating and mowing skills, just two of the jobs to which I was assigned. Each inmate, other than those exempt due to medical conditions, was required to work five days per week. Our time was occupied. We were essentially slave labor. We were paid twelve cents per hour, but effectively we provided labor that would otherwise have to be done by either members of the air force or outside contractors. Either way, the savings were huge since we were essentially free.

As the bus was rolling back into the prison compound, I heard my name being called. "Inmate Gallagher to Baker's office."

What now? I thought. As I made my way to his office area, I was so focused on the mundane events of the day that I was truly clueless as to what was up and what he needed to see me for. One thing I knew was that I had done nothing wrong. With Buck's help, I had learned early about the rules of incarceration and made the commitment that it would be in my best interest to follow those rules strictly.

Following rules was not my strong suit. I preferred to follow only those rules that I was involved in making or that I felt were suited to my needs. Rules in prison were not meant to be broken. I had already come to understand clearly that every choice has a consequence. There was no gain to compound the already dire consequences I was facing and living. My ego and self-centered approach had taken me as low as one could go in society, so now was the time to reevaluate my choices.

"Mr. Baker, what can I do for you?" I asked as I entered his office.

Without looking up or showing any emotion, he said, "Your halfway house has been approved. Currently, your scheduled release date is August 23. Here are the rules of your release. You'll need to make some arrangements. Look these over and get back with me in a day or so." With that, he handed me the release order and poorly photocopied rules. It was my turn to leave.

I could tell that Baker was pleased, if not happy, to be able to grant my request, but he didn't show it. Prisons are odd places. The staff is trained not to get involved and to show little emotion. The inmates are to be kept at bay. The rule is for the staff never to get too close either physically or, more importantly, emotionally.

"Thank you," I said as he pushed the paperwork my way, urging me, without saying so, to leave. While my request for six months of halfway was approved for only five, it was approved. I was ecstatic!

The funny part about prison is that you can't just go out freely and share your joy. There is no cell phone to use, and calls are "collect" only. The more joyous you are about something like a halfway house release, the more the people who will be left behind may become jealous and start thinking of ways to change the outcome or dampen your spirit. So, short of Buck, my cellmate, and Bruce, the guy I was paired with to work each day, I kept the news to myself.

Somehow, I thought this news would be life-changing. Yet I had come to understand that I was not in control. I could immediately rush to trying to live in the future and would quickly find myself losing the benefits of the hard-learned lessons of daily choices. Until that day came, I had no guarantee that my release to the halfway house would be honored. Others had received similar orders, only to find at the last minute that the halfway house was full and their admission was postponed or other issues had risen that caused the release order to be changed. As excited as I would have thought I would have been, I still focused on each day. I had peace in knowing that all was in divine order.

On the day before my scheduled release, I was excited about what the next day would bring for me. After the four o'clock count and dinner that evening, Buck helped me pack up my meager possessions. With the exception of a few books sent from the outside and the clothes I wore into prison, there was nothing else I needed other than my journal. I didn't know if or how it would be helpful in the future, but I had made a commitment to record what happened. As I prepared to leave, my journal was my most precious possession.

As I packed, inmates from around my unit came by to wish me well and see if there was something I was giving away that they would need or want. Since we all made very little and many of them had no money coming in from the outside, the possibility of getting some-thing was certainly appealing. I didn't have much, but I was open to giving what I had. Perhaps someone would get my Ramen Noodles or someone else my toothpaste or some other toiletry. Whatever the item, if someone else could use it, I was delighted to give it away.

As we approached lights out the night before release, I recall Buck asking how I felt. He had been in so long by that time, somewhere between six and seven years, that he couldn't relate to the feeling of something different. And in my case, having been incarcerated for eleven months, I must admit that the feeling was foreign to me as well.

While on one hand, there was anticipation creeping in, in fact, it seemed like just another night. Somehow the idea that I was being released, even if to a halfway house, just didn't seem real. Being incarcerated for eleven months seemed insignificant in relation to the time that most of my fellow inmates had seen. They had been in for a significant part of their lives. Prison and the life it brought had become home, and I couldn't imagine how they might feel about leaving.

Looking back on the experience today, when asked by those who are finding themselves preparing to enter prison, I am often asked what they should expect. My response is consistently, "It will be a life-changing experience. When you emerge, you will never be the same." If eleven months can be life-changing, then for those who find themselves in for years, the experience will be an alteration for not only your life, but for the lives of those who are connected to you.

"Lights out!"

Buck and I soon ended our conversation as I lay on a four-inch plastic foam mattress on a metal bunk bed for what I was hoping would be the last time.

The next morning, as we arose to meet the day, most of my fellow inmates were preparing for another work day in prison, while I was allowed once again to put on civilian clothing as I prepared for departure. Part of me felt it was unreal. Although I had been in prison for only eleven months, it felt like forever. I arrived in prison weighing a little over 200 pounds with a lot of heavy emotional baggage, and I was leaving prison at 175 and much lighter emotionally than when I came. My civilian clothes were a bit baggy. I couldn't have cared less.

As my paperwork was processed for release, I wondered what this new world would hold for me. In eleven months, would things have substantially changed? How would I be treated? Would reentry into society be difficult or easy? What about the people who knew me before prison? Would they see me as a different person? Would they want to have anything to do with me? There were many questions and feelings that morning for me. I was ecstatic about leaving while experiencing a little anxiety about the change.

Just like a child entering the world not knowing what to expect, I entered prison as one person. The person leaving the prison compound was different. True, my personality was the same, but my understanding of the world was different. Most importantly, my understanding of myself was radically different.

I had been incarcerated for eleven months. It was not long by most people's definitions, but it certainly seemed like forever, especially since my world had changed that radically. Eleven months earlier I took twenty-three steps in. As I walked toward the front door and could see out, I reached my hand forward and took twenty-three steps out. Now was the time to turn what seemed to be a negative consequence into what could become positive results.

Eleven months earlier I took twenty-three steps in. As I walked toward the front door and could see out, I reached my hand forward and took twenty-three steps out.

After leaving prison, I examined the world with amazement. I was surprised, even shocked, just how much can change in a fast-paced world in eleven months. Little things that one might take for granted on a daily basis were amazing upon reentry into society. Things like having the freedom to choose what and where you eat were wonderful, especially when that was taken away with incarceration. Going to the mall to purchase new clothing was a wonderful experience, not because of buying something, but because of the freedom to choose. Being free to experience those little choices was wonderful.

Often, with all that I experienced when taking my first steps of semi-freedom, I wondered how difficult it must be for folks like Buck who had been confined for years, isolated from the things that we take for granted daily. Most who are incarcerated find that life upon release is difficult and extremely foreign. When your routine is set daily, your choice of food is made and the clothing you wear is chosen for you, you begin to become what many call "institutionalized." As such, you begin to lose the skills necessary to make effective choices upon release. Eleven months was not long enough to cause that to happen to me, but eleven months was sufficient to make a profound impact on release.

The same is true for people who have created their own prisons. The longer you choose to confine yourself to the prison you're in, the more difficult it is to find ease of life when released. The process of release isn't easy, whether your prison is physical or emotional. There has to be an intention to change, to make different choices, if you want the release to be effective. In the real world, former prisoners return to prison 80 percent of the time because they can't or won't make different choices that could provide them new, more positive lives. The same is true for those who have become "institutionalized" by their emotional choices. Releasing the chains that bind us requires a realized intention to make different, positive choices in order to move into the freedom we desire.

Halfway house was, in fact, prison. Sure there was more freedom, but not much. Every move was monitored, as the expectation was that we were more likely to fail than to succeed. The system is not designed to rehabilitate. Prison is business, and the business model is predicated on having a stable inflow of people to incarcerate. The easiest way to fund the inmate population is to re-incarcerate those who have been there. They know the rules and are easier to work with than introducing someone new, like me, into the system.

As I prepared to re-enter the workforce, I contacted the company I formerly worked for. They were under no obligation to rehire me. In fact, I was considered a high-risk hire as the company policy was to avoid hiring convicted felons. However, this company had what I describe as a "soul." They had compassion, and they knew that I brought one skill to the table that most companies need: I was motivated to succeed. Coming out of prison and knowing that my daily performance would determine my future were immense motivations to make positive choices and prove that the title "convicted felon" meant nothing.

I was hired into direct sales—cold-calling, door-to-door sales. Failure to sell meant failure to eat, and failure was not an option. While most people assume that convicted felons are just looking for another way to cheat and lie, most are looking for a chance to prove their value. I knew that each choice made would be another step toward the "somebody" I already was.

Time seemed to move more quickly after release. I was surprised at how differently the outside world moved. Every day had the same twenty-four hours, the same number of minutes, but the reality of choice, consequence, and result, was magnified. Perhaps that is another reality factor that I was unprepared for, but one that became apparent quickly. When in the turmoil and darkness of our prison, whatever the form, time seems to drag. When we embrace the reality that we can, through our choices, change our reality, we find that the universe speeds positive results, moving us in the direction of our dreams.

Sales did not come quickly, as I had no lead base. That was my responsibility, and I knew that every choice I made would produce some result and each result would be a building block to whatever future I chose to create. While I never had an issue with alcohol, I have to say that I felt much like what I imagined an alcoholic might feel. One day at a time, and the decisions made that day were one more building block in daily and future success. There might have easily been the temptation to claim some form of victimization, but the reality is that most of us, by our choices, make our circumstances. It's hard to be a victim when our choices have created our environment.

Within nine months from prison release to the halfway house, I began to see the manifestation of the daily choices I made. My manager in May of 1997 announced that she wanted to make a change. She wanted to spend more time at home with her young children, and hence, the sales director position became available. Before the announcement was made public, the then-regional president called me and asked if I was ready for more responsibility. Would I be interested in the sales director's role? It was a role I held prior to my incarceration. I was pleasantly surprised by the offer.

While on one hand I was fully prepared to reassume this role, I had no expectation that such a positive result would happen so quickly. Up until that point, I focused each day on what must be done in order to live and achieve the success needed to rebuild my life. While I certainly knew that somehow, someday, I would advance either in sales or management, one thing that continued from my experience in prison was the understanding that the choices made each day were critical.

I have come to understand that I am comfortable living in the future. My time in prison taught me that while dreaming about the future may be fun, the choices made each day are what create the experience of daily living. Tomorrow may be radically different from what we plan or expect. The only thing that we can control is what we choose to do today. Apparently, a sequence of daily choices made over nine months had provided senior management time to regain trust in my focus and ability. This trust provided an opportunity to advance my career.

One choice I made that I don't regret is the choice to be open and honest about who I am today and who I was in my past. My life is an open book. I have come to see not only the beautiful side of the human experience, but also the side that is dark and painful. For whatever reason, many find that it is more comfortable to stay in their own self-defined prisons rather than working through the pain associated with releasing the chains that bind them.

Now, some twelve years later, I have rejoined the corporate world and carried many senior titles for a publicly-held company. I feel uncomfortable, perhaps even like a braggadocio, talking about the success I have achieved following prison. From the depths of my heart, there is no intention to brag. There is nothing to brag about. Yes, it is unusual for a convicted felon to hold a senior position with a public company. The fact that such a position is possible is evidence that the choices I make daily can have positive results even if I am, by law, a convicted felon.

Everything we know now can change in a moment. We are not masters of the future; we only control our choices now. As I speak around the country, invariably I am asked the question, "What did you do to move past the stigma of being a convicted felon? How on earth did you regain success?" The short answer is that every choice has a consequence. I just stayed focused on trying to make choices that would yield positive results.

16

The End Is Just the Beginning

Twenty-three steps from the curb to the door, and on step twenty-four, I took my first step into prison. I took those same twenty-three steps out of prison and emerged a different man. Through losing it all, I accomplished what my mama always told me I could be—I was "somebody!" The funny thing is I learned the lesson the hard way. I was always "somebody"; I just never understood what that meant.

My prison experience was a process. Your "prison" experience can be as well, if you choose to make it so. You can either remain helpless, a victim, stuck in the darkness that your prison really is, or you can become empowered, rise above your current state, and claim the victory that is yours for the taking. How? By the choices you make!

From my twenty-fourth step, every step was a new experience. I was almost like a baby, trusting that where or how I was being led was going to be all right. However, that first step started long before I faced those prison doors. That first step was the one I faced when I was forced to look back at myself with horror and disbelief. The first step was admitting that I had made choices that made me a liar and a thief.

From New York to New Orleans, from Dallas to Denver, wherever I speak, one of the first questions focuses on the "how" of rehabilitation. Most think that rehabilitation is for former inmates, yet it is truly recovery for us all. The "how" is easy. It begins with the first step of admitting that the choices we have made thus far have not gotten us where we want to be.

If you have less than positive results in your life, then you have made less than "good" choices. You are where you are because of the choices you have made. I can hear naysayers exclaiming that I don't know what I'm talking about. "I'm a victim," they often shout. And every time, when they honestly peel back the layers of choices made, they discover that the choices made have a direct effect on where they are today. We all may have been victims as a result of past experiences; however, living in victimization now is a choice. We all have the power to change our lives.

We start by taking that bold step of acknowledging that, if where we are isn't where we want to be, it is because of our choices. That is the first step to empowerment. That is the first step to freedom.

What I've just described is not easy. It is tough. Continuing what you are doing is much easier. After all, doing what you are doing is something that you are comfortable with. I stole money. I am not proud of that fact, but it is a fact nonetheless. Over time, the behavior, which I knew was wrong, was easier to continue than it was to break its cycle and face the pain of having to make better choices.

Help comes only when we face ourselves and the choices we have made and accept responsibility for changing them. We always have the power to improve our lives. The only thing we must do is deal with the pain of change and claim the power of choice. The pain of change is far less than the pain of remaining in desperation.

Generally, at the time we feel most powerless, true change can take place. Long before the sentence of prison, I recognized that my life was unmanageable. Before the true moment of reckoning, I still labored under the false illusion that all was well. The operative word is "illusion." When our choices have become so ineffective that negative consequences are a forgone conclusion, we will at some point recognize that we are not in control.

Often I suspect that people, in our fast-paced, instant-gratification society, expect to make one change and instantly find their lives better. When that doesn't happen, they easily fall back into the pattern of their prison bonds. Nothing worthwhile will happen instantly, especially If the chains that bind us to negative consequences were forged with years of poor choices. Once we accept where we are and how the choices we have made have shaped our current circumstance, we can then, and only then, begin the process of transformation. Once the process of transformation starts in earnest, there is no going back.

But be careful. I know how easy it is to become caught up in those all too familiar patterns. I have to remind myself often that one simple choice earned me a place in prison and if it can happen once, it can happen again. Whether an errant choice earns the consequence of actual prison or a prison of another sort, it is a fact that every choice has a consequence. It is critical to be vigilant when it comes to the choices we make in order to enjoy the positive results that can and do follow.

Once you put forth forward momentum into making a change in your life based on changing your choices and accepting responsibility for where you are, you cannot turn back. While, like birth, there may be pain, intense pain, the reward that comes with making positive choices and enjoying the transformational results that follow can be bliss. Initially, there is sometimes a little sadness leaving the past behind. It sometimes means leaving people behind as you evolve differently from them. It is just part of the process as you move into your life in a positive way.

A word of caution, however, as you begin. The veil of mystery that blocks our understanding of truth is formidable. As humans, we are not meant to understand all. We are here to learn lessons and grow as spiritual beings. Growth comes through experience, and experience is the teacher of lessons. If you find that you get stuck with an idea presented, stop. Ask yourself: what are you feeling blocked by? Then keep an open mind as you know you will know truth.

Many beliefs that we take for granted have been changed by those who opened their minds to other possibilities. For instance, the earth is not flat, as was once believed. Yet, those who held the "flat earth" belief knew that explorers like Columbus were destined to fall off the edge. The visionaries knew better. They stepped out on faith and propelled humanity forward by having a willing spirit and an open mind. The more open you are to change, the easier it is to push toward positive, forward momentum.

Probably the most significant change that solidified my transformation was the complete understanding that, as the song says, "somebody bigger than you and I" was in control. I will never forget the true "miracles" that took place once I released control and turned it over to God. By myself, I was powerless. In fact, the more I tried to control the outcomes, the worse the outcomes or possible outcomes became. Yet, within two weeks of the admission of my guilt, I legitimately had over $500,000 of debt lifted from my shoulders.

I was a believer in God, a universal power, or by whatever name you know the Creator. However, I had never seen the true power of God at work until I released control and allowed God to make perfect order out of chaos. I didn't say that was easy or that the consequences that followed my poor choices were eliminated. They were not. What I experienced was nothing short of multiple "miracles" that paved the way for an effective personal transformation.

Through my choices, I had been blocking the goodness of God. I stood in my own way, not realizing that my obsession with ego and control was the largest impediment to successful living. Today, when faced with people who wonder what they can do to improve their lives, I pose one question—are they willing to release their will and thus open up to the Universe at work?

Some won't admit to a higher power. I understand. Some won't release the need for control—the ego self—to God. That's fine, if you seek less than the best available to you through God's grace. If you want to turn negative consequences into positive results, you must get out of your own way and allow the Spirit to take control. That is easier said than done. I found that I had to reach the point where I understood that I could no longer control my circumstances in order to relinquish control. By the way, none of this means that you avoid the consequences; rather, it means that you set into motion the path to achieving positive results.

This process, which can be time consuming for some, was intense and time constrained for me. I had to fly home knowing that I would admit to my wife, partners, clients, and community that I was a liar and a thief. I was truly powerless and had put myself into a position to have to relinquish control. Through that admission, I faced myself, acknowledging that the illusion of importance I had created was nothing more than an illusion. At that point, I was forced to look in the mirror. The person I could have been, my true nature, had become distorted by the pain of poor choices.

If there is an impediment to achieving positive results in one's life, it is resisting the pain of admitting who we truly are and what we have done to confine ourselves to the prisons we find ourselves in. Whether it is a failed marriage, addiction to drugs, poor relationships with others—whatever the problem that confines us, the challenge is looking inward and facing those choices we have made that contributed to the outcome. While it wasn't easy to look in the mirror and see my reflection, it was incredibly worthwhile.

My marriage failed. That saddens me. I understand why and made a commitment that if I ever was fortunate enough to be blessed with another wife, I would not make the same mistake twice. I broke the trust we had, and when trust is broken, it is often hard, if not impossible, to heal. My choices broke the ties that bound us. My lies and deception made continuing the marriage impossible or highly improbable. My choices broke the bond. From the point when the truth was revealed, my choices solidified whether the marriage would succeed or fail.

Today I am happily married. However, had I taken the victim mentality and never taken a personal inventory of my choices and the consequences that contributed to a failed marriage, I would not have been in a position to be given a second wonderful chance. If you want to release those chains that you feel bound by, take a step forward and look at what you have done to get you there. Then make different choices. As a side note, my wife lovingly reminds me from time to time that I should read what I write and think about what I speak. It's her way of keeping me grounded, of helping me stay present and conscious of the choices I make today.

At a recent seminar, a participant asked, "What did the people you stole money from think of you?"

"They thought I was great until I admitted what I did. After that, well . . . to say they didn't like me was a bit of an understatement." The admission of truth was difficult, painful, and fearful. Yet, by admitting the truth, even with the painful consequences that followed, I felt a feeling of relief and freedom. I knew, in time, I would recover from the pain of rejection I brought on by my choices.

Even today, I do not hide my past. I have come to believe that being willing to speak the truth, even when the truth is ugly, is a forward step that has opened many doors and created powerful positive results. I am not proud of being labeled a "convicted felon." Yet, had I hidden that from others for these many years following prison, I can assure any reader that I would have been skewered and had the fact used against me. I do not flaunt my past, but I do not hide it. It is a part of me, and by being willing to admit my past choices and consequences, I have found power in keeping myself grounded. I have also found that people are respectful of one who doesn't hide from the truth.

When you are willing to accept responsibility for your choices and your actions and admit them to those who have been harmed, you are taking a huge step forward in your own personal transformation. Here's the hard part: Just like the law of gravity, you cannot selectively choose who this applies to. If you truly want freedom from your own personal prison, you must be brutally honest with yourself and honest with others.

Recently, I was writing about white-collar crime and came across a story about a man who admitted guilt to one crime, thinking that once he faced the consequences of what he admitted guilt to, it would be over. Well, there's an old song that says, "What you do in the dark will be brought to the light." In his case, other crimes then surfaced. The outcome? If he had been willing to "fess up" the first time around, he would likely have been well on the way by now to completing his sentence and moving his life forward. However, in his case, the second wave of consequences for his newfound crimes created more severe consequences that will take him years to overcome.

From experience, I can declare that my willingness to make the choice of being completely honest at first made all the difference. Again, it didn't mean the consequences didn't exist—they did—but I am confident that they were far less severe than they could have been had I made a different choice. Every choice has a consequence, and I am so happy that, by the grace of God, I made the right choice here.

Being honest with those who I had harmed and being willing to do whatever, legally, it took to make restitution were huge in the choices category. While it is hard to admit that you are wrong—at least, it was for me—what was more difficult was being willing to make restitution.

There are so many times when I hear people who have admitted wrong expect to be forgiven without trying to make their poor choices right. It doesn't work that way. If I make bad choices and then assume that somehow I have no responsibility for making correct choices, then

I have missed the point and will find that I will remain stuck in the prison walls I have created.

Fixing every mistake is not always possible. In some cases, we just don't know who our choices have touched and the impact that our choices may have made on others. No one expects perfection when trying to make amends. In my case, however—at least, for the direct choices of lying and theft—it was clear who I had harmed and what needed to be done to correct that.

Another question arose at a conference where I made an address: "What has been the hardest part of your personal journey?"

I get questions all the time, and most fall into a similar pattern so that now I can anticipate them. This question gave me pause, and in a moment of silence the answer came to me clearly. "Powerful question," I responded. "The hardest part of my personal journey is recognizing that it isn't over. It's knowing that I have to face my defects of character daily and be vigilant in my efforts spiritually to grow past them. It's the recognition that I must keep my ego in check and always be mindful that I am not in control. It's asking God to give me the strength to be helpful to others and not hurtful to myself."

If you find that you've been unfaithful in a marriage, you might find it easy to be unfaithful again. If you have a problem with alcohol, you might find it easy to take a drink again. If you find it easy to lie, then you might find that lying becomes an easy out. If you once learn to steal, you might find that stealing can become natural. Behavior that can imprison you once can imprison you again unless you maintain a vigilant eye on the choices you make daily. Know that one misstep can lead to disastrous consequences.

Behavior that can imprison you once can imprison you
again unless you maintain a vigilant eye on the choices you make daily.
Know that one misstep can lead to disastrous consequences.

Following my release from prison, life has not been a bed of roses. Sometimes I get the feeling that since I have seen extraordinarily positive results, people sometimes think that it just all fell into place. They believe that it was easy. That is far from the truth. I have been promoted, demoted, and re-promoted, and I faced many times the need to admit mistakes—to admit my shortcomings. It is no easier now than it was in years past. The only difference is, now I know the power of choice. I realize that I am less than perfect and that my willingness to admit my human faults is just part of the "choices" step to personal growth and positive results. Now I have peace in knowing that even when facing difficult times, there is something positive to learn.

Peace is obtained when we know what is going on—when we have gained greater awareness. Unfortunately, most people have only a limited awareness, if any, of their roles in co-creation. By co-creation, I mean that, since our choices create our circumstances, we have a direct connection with where we are by the choices we make. By being consciously aware of our roles as co-creators in our earthly plight, we come to an awareness of the "big picture." Hence, when someone treats us unkindly, when harmless circumstances erode into an altercation, or when things just don't seem to be going our way, we can stop and understand that what's happening is for our higher learning. At that point, the momentary impact of the event becomes clearer and more meaningful.

Up until 1990, which was the better part of my adult life, I thought I was in control. I believed in a higher power, but allowed my ego to grow to a point that I thought I was the smartest guy in the room. Now I know better.

My life had become so out of control that nothing I could do would make it right. And now, almost two decades later, people who find themselves in their own prisons seek advice on how to turn their negative consequences into positive results. The answers are laced throughout this book.

The hardest part is the beginning, for it is best to take responsibility for our lives as they are. Blaming others or events for our predicament does no good other than to placate our ego. All of the events in our past—everything leading up to the present moment—serve only to offer an explanation of why we act as we do. Those events do not excuse what we do. They are not responsible for our choices—we are. The sooner we recognize that simple fact, the quicker we can turn the tide to achieving positive results. When we think about it, every circumstance of our lives is something we created. Therefore, our state of happiness and well-being rests with us. If you are experiencing negative consequences from your choices, as I did, remember that you made the choices.

I'm not sure most people want to know the truth about happiness or the way to achieve the positive results in life. It's much easier to allow our egos to blame others for our misfortune. What we don't realize when blaming others for our choices is that we are, in fact, giving our power away. Controlling ourselves is easier when we come to claim our own power. Accepting responsibility for our choices empowers us to a degree that brings us peace regardless of our circumstances.

In my case, I came to my senses. The entire process was a spiritual awakening. From admitting guilt, to making restitution, to entering prison—the process served as a way to change me, to allow me to become what my mother predicted so many years earlier. The awakening allowed me to be "somebody." Furthermore, a more important facet of the journey has emerged; the part that allows for the truths learned to be shared.

Regardless of what people call me or the circumstances that I might find myself in, the fact is that I can choose peace and calm regardless of how others are acting. If happiness is dependent on the way others act, then as humans, we are giving away our power. Turning power over to other people empowers them to determine how we feel. The truth is, that choice is yours. By your choices, you are empowered. By your choices, you can break the chains that bind you. By your choices, you can find joy and happiness.

> By your choices, you are empowered. By your choices, you can break the chains that bind you. By your choices, you can find joy and happiness.

Happiness is not determined by others, but by you. How often we neglect this truth. We can either keep it for ourselves or give it to others. Rather than vesting our good with others, we should take possession of what we already own, and we own the power to choose. Choice was given to us by God in spirit form and passed on during our incarnation. The power that comes from "choice" seems to be hidden from view for most of us. Sometimes the obvious is the hardest to see until we have that spiritual awakening that allows the veil to be removed. It is clear now that growth and happiness come when we put our energy and time into accomplishing our life's purpose. The only way to accomplish what we came here to do is through the choices we make daily, each one a step on the path.

Spiritual understanding is a process. You cannot get it from reading a book or hearing a speaker or listening to a recording, although I do all three of those just to continue the spiritual process. Those provide the opportunity to help interpret life events. However, understanding comes from living, from experience, and from learning the lessons life's events offer you. The book or lecture may give tremendous insight. I wouldn't be writing this book if I didn't feel there was something to be gained. Yet, I know that no amount of knowledge will sustain your spirit. Right action, a by-product of experience, is necessary if knowledge, from wherever it is obtained, is to come alive.

If it is possible to disassociate yourself and look at your own life objectively, amazing truths unfold. All I knew at the time was "fear," fear of facing the creation I crafted. I did not know the outcome. I sensed a part of me would die, and there was some truth to that fear. Now, however, I see the benefit of fear rightly used. Fear can propel us forward by making right choices and seeking higher truth.

Before I took those twenty-three steps, I lived life as an illusion. After I became 11642-058, I understood that the choices I made served only to create an illusion and illusions eventually fade to reality. I didn't like the reality I had created.

Before I took those twenty-three steps, I thought I made good choices. For a time, I enjoyed positive results from the choices I made. After I became 11642-058, I had a clearer understanding about choices and their consequences. I came to know that we are in control of the way we experience those consequences and create the consequences by the choices we make.

Before I took those twenty-three steps, I thought I was success-ful. After I became 11642-058, I realized what success truly meant. Success is not defined by the external, the material, the title. True success comes from the impact you have on the lives of others. When your choices empower others to grow and experience positive results, then you can claim success.

With this end, perhaps you can find your beginning. So, look past the illusion, make good choices, and claim your success. This is the path to claiming the "somebody" you already are!

17

Points to Ponder

———◆———

I took twenty-three steps into federal prison. When I took those same twenty-three steps out, my life had changed. I appeared physically the same, but my inner understanding was different. I was transformed and had learned some valuable lessons that continue to guide me today. Here are my twenty-three truths and points to ponder. I hope that through this book, you too, may uncover the keys to unlock your prison and find a happier life. You have the power to unlock those chains that bind you and turn adversity into opportunity. You have the power of choice.

1. Every choice we make in life will have either a negative consequence or a positive result. The outcome we receive is directly connected to the choices we make. As we live our outcomes, the more aware we become of how our choices impact the results we live, the greater power we have to produce the outcomes we desire. Choices made without self-integrity or ethics result in negative results, while choices made with self-integrity result in positive results. My life demonstrates both extremes.

2. We are given the creative power to manifest our present and our future, just as we have created our past. It isn't

fate that determines our future. We choose our future by the choices we make today. If we don't like the present we are living or desire a more positive future, we can create it—the power is ours. Our ability to break the chains from the past allows us to live in our present and choose to create the future we desire.

3.   Mirror, mirror, on the wall—is what we've created reality at all? Sometimes we believe the illusions in our lives are reality. When we find the courage to look in the mirror, we find that the reflection is the person controlling the illusions. When we are willing to look past the illusions we've created, we can then find the reality hidden beneath our well-crafted surface. By facing the mirror, perhaps we can grasp the truth of who we are. Then we can begin the process of freeing ourselves from the chains that bind us and keep us captive in the prisons we've created. Only by choosing to move past the illusion and accepting the reality can we truly choose our freedom. The key to unlocking the chains is accepting responsibility for what we've created and knowing that we have the ability to change it through the choices we make.

4.   How can I change my life? Often it takes hitting rock bottom in order to be forced to recognize the need for change. Hitting rock bottom is like being in complete darkness, experiencing complete aloneness, and having complete awareness that there is no way out if we continue making the choices we've made in the past. Frequently, when we hit rock bottom, we comprehend the depravity of our life. Then, if we choose, we move forward into grace. At that point, we are truly

empowered to seek the way out. To hit rock bottom is truly a gift. And, for some of us, only then do we accept the responsibility for where we are and recognize that changing our choices is the only way to improve our lives.

5.   When we live in illusions, we often stand in judgment of other people's choices. When we judge other people, we maintain our illusion of personal goodness. Illusions created by judgments keep us from observing life and cause us to miss our own life lessons. When we release those judgments, we come closer to seeing the truth and are free to evolve positively in our journeys.

6.   We are spiritual beings living in a physical world. Often, the truth of our existence is hidden by living our day-to-day humanness. There are no mistakes, only opportunities to learn and grow. Even in the worst of situations, we can grow spiritually. We can use every circumstance for growth and good based on the choices we make. When I learned to release myself from judgment for my choices, I awakened to the power of spirit moving in my life. Fortunately, to receive a greater understanding, all we need to do is turn in the right direction.

7.   Through our darkest moment, we find the greatest gifts. By admitting weakness, we find our greatest strength. By exposing the reality of who we are and what we have done, we find our greatest acceptance. So often I hear people ask about challenges I face, having served time in prison. By being open about who I am and the choices I have made, I have found that my conviction

is not an impediment, but rather a source of power to help others along their journey.

8. Breaking through the prisons that bind us is often done one step at a time. From the time I initially exposed the choices I made and who I had become, the road to recovery took time and effort. The initial breakthrough may appear to happen quickly, but maintaining freedom takes time. There is not a day that goes by that I do not think, in some form, about the choices that I made and how those choices affected me. Being aware daily of the fact that every choice has a consequence and, therefore, making right choices are the keys to unlocking the doors to freedom.

9. Being "somebody" isn't defined by our outer material trappings. Rather, being "somebody" is defined by using our talents and gifts in a constructive, helpful, and productive way. What you think, you are. Therefore, being "somebody" is only a state of mind. Living in our own self-integrity and allowing that to be present in every aspect of our lives creates a framework for who we are and who we become. I have found that the more I am willing to give to others, the more a "somebody" I am.

10. The journey to freedom may not be an easy one, but running away from it only prolongs the agony. People approach me following a presentation and ask about the journey—what was involved and how they might find freedom. When they hear my reply, their challenge becomes whether or not they are willing to make the choices necessary to achieve what they are looking

for. To find true freedom, we must take dominion over our lives. The life I live is an expression of the choices I make. In order to achieve harmony, happiness and health, I must be willing to take control of my choices and make decisions that will open the door to freedom.

11. Everything in life has a divine order. Often, our choices confuse the order. There is a way through every situation. When we release control and allow the spiritual power of life to take hold, all will be restored to order. By making right choices, right action and consequences will follow. That does not mean the road to divine order will be smooth. We may not get what we think we want, but in the end, we will receive what we need. In my case, the outcome was better than I imagined.

12. Learning and understanding is a process. If we expect to make a right choice and "all will be well," we haven't fully grasped the process. Understanding comes from living, from experiencing, and from learning the lessons life's events offer us. The choices we make offer the opportunity to learn. As we see the consequences from our choices, we begin to connect the dots. We learn that we control the outcome. We control the lives we live. Right action, a by-product of experience, is necessary if knowledge of our choices is to come alive.

13. For something to be born anew, there must be a change and a cleansing. When a baby is born, there is pain, pressure, and discomfort; finally, the cord is cut. We call this the miracle of birth. For change to occur, we need the transformation of birth in many areas of our lives. So many wish to avoid the pain,

pressure, and discomfort, opting instead to live lives in an old, stale way. When, however, we find ourselves in an uncomfortable situation, if we're aware, we may come to understand that something new and better is on the horizon.

14. We will influence the world; how is determined by the choices we make. Wherever we are, whatever we do, the choices we make have impact. The simple choices we make and the way we live our lives has greater influence on others than we can imagine.

15. Our life purpose isn't a destination. It is a journey fraught with many experiences designed to give us what we need ultimately to succeed in this lifetime. I have often been asked, knowing what I know now, would I have done what I did again? "Of course not," is my response. However, the experience of being in prison was profound. That experience, coupled with many others, has provided a framework for living my life's purpose. If I can somehow help others understand the power of choice and learn how to overcome obstacles and thereby live a fuller and richer life, then the experience and journey will have been worthwhile.

16. The longer we choose to confine ourselves to prison, the more difficult reentry into life will be. We must have the will to leave prison behind and embrace and live in freedom. We know that many things can imprison us. Our prisons could be failed relationships, anger over a perceived past wrong, alcohol, smoking, excessive use of anything. Prisons come in all sizes and

shapes and don't require iron doors to make them real. True freedom comes when we understand that we can have a better life. We are empowered to break the chains that bind, and that begins with intention.

17. Dreaming about the future may be fun, but the choices made each day create the experience of daily living, and the experience of daily living creates the foundation for the future. Tomorrow may be radically different from what we plan or expect, but if our foundation is securely based on the choices we make, we can deal with the unexpected. In reality, the only thing that we can control Is what we choose to do today. Choose wisely, because tomorrow may not be what you expected.

18. By being transparent about the reality of who we are and our experiences, we give permission to other people to do the same. Openness is empowering. Often, I've been asked about my choice to be open about my past. Frankly, I've found that two things happen when I elect to be transparent about who I am. First, being open removes attacks. I have made mistakes. I admit it. I have spent time in prison. I admit it. When I am open about who I am, I become real, and acceptance follows. But, more importantly, when I am real, I allow others to be real as well, and that creates a true connection when openness and honesty can follow.

19. If I have less than positive results in my life, then I have made less than "good" choices, either consciously or subconsciously. I am where I am because of the

choices I have made. This step in the process tends to garner the most controversy. So many people want to hold on to their "victimhood." I hear so often that a personal "prison" must be the fault of someone else. We are responsible for where we are in our lives. Our choices have brought us to the point we are today. By writing this book, I am well on my way to taking the steps I need to creating a bright future. I took twenty-three steps. It is my hope that you can learn from my experience and avoid some of the pain of self-inflicted "prisons."

20. There is pain with change, and sometimes the only thing we can do in the midst of the pain is to claim the power of choice. It is important to remember that the pain doesn't last forever and that the pain of change is far greater than the pain of remaining in desperation. The pain of prison was unpleasant, to say the least. But it was a pain that I needed to go through in order to learn that all choices have consequences, and I was empowered to make life different simply by making better choices. If life is giving you pain, consider the choices you are making now. Ask yourself if they are creating more pain, or if they are creating a foundation for true success.

21. Once the process of transformation starts in earnest, there is no going back because going back would be more uncomfortable than going forward. A baby being born cannot reverse the process. The same is true in our adult lives. While there may be discomfort in a transformative process, the fact remains that the process must be complete. Of course, outcome from the trans-

formation process will either be positive or negative based on choices. Some may argue, that results are not the function of choices, but at the deepest level what we choose defines us.

22. Initially, there is sadness in leaving the past behind. Often, we must leave people behind as we evolve differently from them. That is part of the process as we move into a new life. I clearly made some bad choices in my life. There were people who, once they knew of my actions, left me behind. Likewise, there were people who I left behind. In both cases, our relationships no longer served where we were and who we were becoming. If there is one obstacle to claiming your success, often I find that it is the unwillingness to leave the comfort of those you are connected with. If you choose to move your life into positive territory, then you must be willing to leave past choices behind.

23. Other people do not determine happiness; happiness is determined by our intentions and our choices. Every choice has a consequence. I could have wallowed in the illusion that somehow convicted felons are marked for life and live a life of pain and unhappiness. I deserve better. Don't you? The first step to claiming a new you, to claiming your happiness, to claiming the joy that can be yours daily, begins with one step.

Choices . . . step one. Choices . . . step two. Choices . . . step three. Choices . . . step four. Each choice we make and each step we take provide the foundation for our future. Every choice has a consequence. Wherever you are right now, regardless of the circumstance, you can turn adversity into opportunity. The power is yours. Look past the illusion, make wise choices, and claim the success that is already yours!

Afterword

There is no obstacle that cannot be overcome. That statement is powerful, but the power of the human spirit transcends anything placed before it. The power to achieve and the power to overcome grow from internal desire. Whether the desire to achieve, succeed, become empowered, or help others, whatever our heart desires can become reality if only we focus our energy and choices in that direction.

Everyone, at some point in life, will face challenges. Some may feel them insignificant, and others consider life challenges as major adversity. With over a half-century behind me, I have concluded that one fact is sure: we cannot with accuracy predict the future. What we may face or will face will be a test, and the choices that we make as a result will, in many ways, define us. The true test of who we are is carved out of how we deal with life's adversities.

I have been asked many questions in the years following my prison experience. In this book, I resisted spending too much time answering them, especially those that deal with success following prison. I suppose I had the feeling that talking too much about my success following prison would be perceived as bragging, and I, in no way, felt like what I had done or accomplished should be touted. In reality, all I had done was nothing more than what anyone could have done if only attention was focused and positive choices made.

One question consistently arises: "How did you get a job following prison?" Every choice has a consequence. The choices I made before entering prison set the stage for employment to follow. Several people, namely Brent Heffron, Ken Stephens, David Whitener and Frank Stewart, executives with Stewart Enterprises, knew that I had made poor choices in my past and might face prison, yet these men also had the insight to understand that if I was allowed to use God-given gifts in a productive way, there might be a positive outcome. I was a contract employee with a Stewart Enterprises facility before my sentence, and because of the work and contribution I made then, I was re-employed following prison, though in a lesser capacity.

I want to be clear here because many who read could become confused. There are no free lunches. Whether the adversity you might face results in a loss of your marriage, family, possessions, or your freedom, as mine did, the reality is hope. The choices you make while in the midst of your deepest, darkest despair, some call this the dark night of the soul, may be the very choices that bring you the greatest reward in the future. I quickly learned that good choices have power to bring eventual positive outcomes.

There is another aspect of my journey that often is misunderstood or goes undetected. I believe that you cannot be hurt or held hostage by what is clearly in the light for all to see. Many of the people I knew in federal prison had said, upon their release, that they were leaving their hometown area and starting fresh—putting the past behind them. I chose a different path. Since release, I have been open and willing to discuss my past poor choices and never tried to hide the fact that I had been convicted of a felony. I am not defined by my conviction. I was convicted for a past series of poor choices, but I am not defined by a label. I am confident that your success in life has everything to do with the choices you make today, not the realities of your past. "You may have made a mistake, but YOU are not a mistake." Those words are profound. Repeat them to yourself if need be. Let them sink deep into your soul. You are not a mistake.

Success or failure is just part of the journey we call life. Many I have been privileged to speak to have commented on my journey and the inspiration it gives them. I have been blessed that I took those twenty-three steps and from them learned life lessons that have empowered me and can empower you as well. If you read this book as more than a story, you'll come to understand that the secrets contained herein can transform your life or the lives of those you know. When you transform adversity into opportunity and then into success, you become truly empowered.

About the Author

Chuck Gallagher, business executive, author, and speaker, understands the challenges of business from both a growth and ethics perspective. As a professional speaker, Chuck has been featured in *Business Week*, *New Perspectives*, and other print publications as well as served as a guest on CNN, CBS, NPR, and various TV stations.

Gallagher came from humble beginnings, being raised by a single parent in the projects. More recently, however, he has led his region in over $40 million in sales with 125 sales representatives in a public company. Now he is Chief Operating Office in a national private company. Gallagher is a sought-after speaker, as his programs help employees increase their performance and skills while realizing the ramifications of their ethical choices.

At twenty-six, Gallagher became tax partner at a CPA firm and was one of only three CPAs in the country asked to testify before the U.S. House Ways and Means Committee on a new employee benefits provision of the tax law. He has authored numerous articles for national publications and has developed several continuing professional education (CPE) seminars, which he has taught with passion and a flair that audiences loved.

In the middle of a rising career, Gallagher lost everything because he made some bad choices. He has since rebuilt his career and is now enjoying the success he once did. With more vulnerability than the average keynoter, Gallagher shares with his audiences his life journey, the consequences of his unethical choices, and how life gives you a second chance when you make the right choices. *Second Chances* outlines the journey down and the recovery back, demonstrating that you can turn adversity into opportunity and then success.

Having captured the attention of audiences from coast to coast, Chuck is an inspirational motivational speaker with a dynamic choices and ethics message. As a business ethics speaker and sales motivational speaker, Chuck's business and personal experiences over thirty years provide a powerful framework for presentations, workshops, and consulting. Chuck understands the business and ethical challenges facing organizations today, whether corporate, government, or associations.

For information about Chuck's presentations, coaching, or training programs contact him at chuck@chuckgallagher.com or (828) 244-1400.